A Rage For Rock Gardening

*The story of Reginald Farrer, gardener,
writer and plant collector*

A hundred years ago, British gardening underwent a revolution, as the garden changed from being a diversion of dukes to the hobby of millions.

Few figures were more prominent in this renaissance than Reginald Farrer, the man who put a rockery in every back garden.

Farrer was tormented by physical and emotional misfortune. Yet, in the realm of horticulture, his many faults were turned to advantages, and he became one of the greatest plant-hunters, collecting new species from the mountains of far-off Tibet and China.

Through the influence of his extraordinary books, Farrer did for gardening what, half a century later, Elizabeth David did for cookery, changing everything for ever.

A RAGE FOR ROCK GARDENING

THE STORY OF REGINALD FARRER, GARDENER, WRITER AND PLANT COLLECTOR

NICOLA SHULMAN

 SHORT BOOKS

First published in 2002 by
Short Books
15 Highbury Terrace
London N5 1UP

This paperback edition 2003
10 9 8 7 6 5 4 3 2 1

A CIP catalogue record for this book
is available from the British Library.

ISBN 1-904095-47-X

Printed in Great Britain by
Bookmarque Ltd, Croydon, Surrey

For Constantine

Dear, I know nothing of
Either, but when I try to imagine a faultless love
Or the life to come, what I hear is the murmur
Of underground streams, what I see is a limestone
landscape.

In Praise of Limestone, W.H. Auden

Balliol College, Oxford, 1899. Benjamin Jowett, the reforming Master of the college, was six years dead. Under him, it had changed from an essentially religious institution, supplying curates to the cloth, into a sort of arsenal for the Empire, specialising in the manufacture of political and civic giants: viceroys, archbishops, cabinet ministers were now manoeuvred out of its gates and into their appointments in the key positions of power. After him, there came a generation of undergraduates with quite different intentions. Although these were mostly born in 1880, it could be said of them that they were the first to manifest that distinctly post-Victorian quality, an antipathy to growing up. Notions of duty and worldly ambition repelled them somewhat. They were venturesome: for them, the memorable undergraduates of the day were not the ones with their noses aimed at the cabinet, but those on whom the greatest gifts of nature and fortune sat most lightly.

Two figures emerge to refine the type: Aubrey Herbert and Raymond Asquith. They were creatures of extraordinary mystique, whose well-bred ease, by its nature unattainable through effort, inspired in their peers a hero-worship that long outlasted the age of impressionability. As an old man, the memoirist Lawrence Jones recalled his first meeting with Asquith:

A most vivid picture of my freshman days is the sudden appearance in my rooms, one winter's night, of a new face, framed in the upturned collar of a fur coat, the most beautiful, subtle and distinguished young man's counte-nance that I had ever set eyes upon.

Asquith's beauty was his least advantage. The Regius Professor of Greek took off his hat to him if they passed in the street. He also was witty, cool, discriminating; the dazzle of his urbanity was discernible from yards away, amazing to provincial eyes. He acknowledged his gifts for the pleasure they brought him, but largely despised the worldly success they could procure, in politics or in commerce. As the son of H.H. Asquith, the coming man of the Liberal party, he was held to know what he was talking about, and his posture was widely adopted by his contemporaries, to whom it conveyed no whiff of reaction, but freedom and self-determination.

The case of Herbert, the son of the Earl of Carnarvon, is less straightforward. Later he would be a hero of the Gallipoli campaign and twice refuse the throne of Albania; now he was a dishevelled boy, half-blind, not altogether beautiful; and yet he had personal magnetism that produced in the susceptible a more intoxicated response than the admiration that was due to his friend. To judge from accounts, susceptibility to his charm was general but in some, like John Buchan, who later wrote *Greenmantle* about him, it turned into something like love.

In memoirs where Asquith and Herbert are featured together, there sometimes appears, very much lower down on the programme, the name of Reginald Farrer. He was also at Balliol, but he had not come in on such a good ticket. If it had been his face peeping out from the fur collar on that winter's night, it would have left

Jones with an altogether different memory for his scrap-book. For a start, he would have had to take a step back and look down, because Farrer was short, almost to dwarfishness. He had his mother's heaviness, and a face like proving dough, with dark hair growing from a low forehead and a hare-lip that took refuge behind a moustache as yet too weak in growth to disguise it. Like many ugly people he had nice eyes: dark, and shining, according to his younger cousin Osbert Sitwell, with a 'particular and urgent light that is only to be noticed in the eyes of the deaf, or in those who experience some physical difficulty in utterance'. Sitwell mischievously claimed to find this unaccountable, as the Farrer he knew had no hesitation in speaking. He meant to imply that the problem was, if anything, the reverse.

But it can be accounted for. Farrer's hare-lip was the external symptom of a worse affliction. He had been born with a cleft palate. In early childhood several operations were performed upon the little boy by physicians who still half-believed that the condition was caused by maternal frights (and indeed Farrer's pregnant mother had been surprised by a chimney sweep). The standard procedures involved hot tongs, sulphuric acid and metal bridles; but in spite of them he could not speak intelligibly, and until he was fifteen the only person who could properly understand him was his mother.

The consequences of this defect on his life and personality are hard to enumerate, but three at least are obvious. Firstly, the pain and tedium of his childhood taught him to endure physical hardship, and his own hardly-won toughness gave him a lifelong intolerance of frailty in himself or others. Secondly, he was left with the characteristic speaking voice of cleft palate: a shallow bugling screech, like wind through cracked metal. According to a contemporary treatise on cleft palate, 'It is scarcely possible to estimate the number of adults who are practically excluded from society by this distressing deformity,' for this often resulted in a refusal to speak at all. Lastly, his condition prevented him from going to school, and so he enjoyed a great deal more home life than was usual for a boy of his type.

Farrer was born in London, but home was the family estate, at Clapham in North Yorkshire, to which he was heir. The Ingleborough Estate, for so it is called, was acquired for its shooting in the late eighteenth century, with money earned from the successful family law firm and perceptively invested. Its purchase was the first step in a process wherein the Farrers, or this branch at least, turned from lawyers – to the Crown, and indeed to everybody or any institution of consequence – to gentlemen, thereby exchanging their position of unique power in Britain to one of moderate influence in the Skipton area. This was viewed by all as an advance.

By the time Reginald was born the process was complete. His father, James Anson Farrer, was indisputably a gentleman: he had a large estate, was high sheriff of Yorkshire, had several times been Liberal MP for Skipton and was a prolific writer of books that nobody read. If he was a remote figure in his older son's early life, the slack was taken up by his wife, Bessie, who set then a standard of interest and attention that may later have led to unreasonable expectations. Reginald's mother was a woman of few but fervent interests, and her chief love was the Church. Many are the plaques in Clapham church commemorating her acts of largesse, which included, though there is no plaque for this, the provision of a meek and attentive congregation from the ranks of her husband's tenantry.

Her other passion was her sickly oldest son. Seeing as she had the ordering of his education and upbringing largely to herself, there was no reason to suppose the two might be incompatible; and it has been suggested that she cherished clerical ambitions for Reginald. Whether she did or not, the world in which he grew up, with the predictable fusses about his delicate health making it even more difficult to get away, was one of missionary meetings and temperance rallies and endless family prayers, where, wrote his cousin, 'you could have possessions so long as you did not enjoy them, and where every Sunday dragged after it a weary, weekly train of charitable village functions, jumble sale or jamboree.'

The shock of Oxford on a boy like this would have been immediate, if only because he could do what he wanted without his mother finding out. But Oxford showed him other systems and other ways of life, undreamed of in the Ingleborough philosophy. The curriculum itself (for Literae Humaniores, or Greats, the degree read by Farrer) was no longer required to support Church doctrine, and the reading list would now have included such corrosive elements as Locke and

John Stuart Mill. But the effect of even the reading list was probably less pronounced than that of his new friends, and particularly of Aubrey Herbert. Herbert combined, with the more usual talent for breaking college crockery, a rapturous humour, an effortless verbal inventiveness and a manner, with his friends, of having no reserve at all. He drew confidences as easily as he shared them and possessed the gift of making his friends feel prized and understood, with all the unmeant treachery entailed in that bequest. To Farrer, raised in cautious doctrines of forbearance and discretion, he seemed the personification of joy. He put Aubrey at the centre of his life, now and always. But Farrer took everything personally, and Herbert intended nothing personally – his own romance was with causes, it turned out, and he had no introspection in him – and the result was rows, then brooding and self-recrimination, but on Farrer's part only. He wrote to Herbert, 'You don't have... my ineffaceable memory and my sense of the indelible permanence of things done and said once in a fit of some kind,' and it was true. These episodes left Herbert's memory unmarked.

Where Farrer stood in the eyes of his contemporaries is not wholly apparent. There was in his day a circle of privilege at Balliol, and into this he was certainly brought, but as a guest, not a resident. His parents ensured he had neither the money nor the freedom of movement for any such domicile. When merry groups of young men went off for study parties in Lord Carnarvon's villa in Portofino, Farrer sat up in Ingleborough and wished he was there. He attracted some sympathy: L. E. Jones remembers the general embarrassment when, during a parlour game, Reginald's 'pygmy body' was described in his presence as 'the soul's dark cottage, battered and decayed', but that this was unusual, because 'the normal man's reaction to his physical abnormalities was to feel chivalrous.' He added that the insult was probably far more acceptable than the pity it engendered, and in this he was right. What Farrer wanted was admiration, and plenty of it.

How this might be come by was a matter of consuming interest for the tenant of the battered cottage. His friends could not then know that he would become one of the last of the world's great plant collectors, that he would make possible a new kind of gardening, and invent a new kind of language to describe it; that he would influence the appearance of gardens and the style of garden writing for generations. And if they had, who can say they would have been impressed? They were not impressed by Downing Street.

Farrer's solution was to set himself up as a member of the intellectual elite. He cultivated his prose style and published a play in verse. He developed an elaborate, epigrammatic way of speaking, and an attitude of gorgonising contempt for anyone hesitant, or bungling or 'chivalrous' as was the hapless Jones, who found himself silenced with snorts of derision every time he ventured a remark. He even started his own debating society, the Ganymede – a staggering act of overreach for someone who three years before had been effectively a mute. But a success was made of it, and by the end of his Oxford career he had grown a reputation as a fearsome intellect and a witty and fascinating speaker – which then was severely frosted by his examination results: a third in Greats, to add to his second in moderations*.

One can speculate on the reasons for such a dismal

*The examination taken at the end of the second year of study show. He had been quite ill with diphtheria earlier that year (1901). This was also the year he set up his own alpine nursery at Ingleborough, and became the precocious recipient of medals at shows locally and in London. They may have been achieved at the expense of his studies. But the possibility must be entertained that he was not as clever as he thought; a most unwelcome explanation and one that must have crossed his own mind. Asquith and Herbert both took firsts.

For most people the condition of their university degree is a matter of passing concern, but for Farrer it was a heavy addition to the burden of what he already had to prove. There is every reason to suppose, as some of those who knew him did, that this was the event that turned the issue of his cleverness into a cause; one which he prosecuted with inconsolable ferocity over a writing career of twenty years. He produced books – novels, poetry, garden books in several volumes, travel books, translations, verse plays in French and English – at the rate of two or three and, once, four a year; and the business of all of them was to importune the world with proof upon proof of their author's intellectual capabilities, until it gave in at last and concurred.

An opportunity came soon after leaving Oxford. Aubrey Herbert's mother, Elsie Carnarvon, shared with Bessie Farrer a tendency to oppressive maternal doting; but her attentions took a more enterprising form and, after much pushing, she succeeded in getting her son a job as attaché to the British Embassy in Tokyo. He asked Farrer to go out and join him, along with some other Balliol friends. For once, Farrer's parents let him go. 'Am delighted at the idea of Japan,' he wrote to Herbert, 'we could take a house or something perhaps & I should be able to have a tremendously busy time, plant-hunting, & I would stay till early summer – or until we quarrelled quite too desperately.' In the event, Farrer set up his own establishment in Tokyo, probably to avoid rows, and travelled out of it, both alone and in company with Gertrude Bell and her brother Hugo, into other parts of Japan and Korea. He did collect plants: the business of collecting had been serious for him since, at thirteen, he had been the one to find *Arenaria gothica* growing on the cliffs at Ingleborough, where it had never been found before, and reported it in a letter to the *Journal of Botany*. However, although Bell describes him as coming down from Mount Fuji carrying a 'rose pink cyprodium' [sic] he had found on its flanks, no accounts of this trip suggest an organised intention to collect the flora of Japan. Nothing here in nature excited him as much as what he saw in Japanese art; and even horticulturally speaking, it was art, in the form of the close attentions of Japanese nurserymen and garden makers to their natural material, that most drew his admiration.

In Japan, then, in 1903, he visited Japanese gardens and immediately recognised them as quite alien to anything he had yet seen represented under that name, and superior. He became at once a proselyte for the concentrated beauty of the Japanese method, and a scourge of the pitiful English imitations at that time proliferating in the gardens of the rich. Other than this, he went shopping – he loved shopping and had a particular weakness for textiles and elaborate costumes, liking to wear them himself – and visited the usual sites and attractions. His route did not deviate much from the shallow groove already worn by Western visitors, and it is perhaps characteristic of him to suppose his impressions would be of interest to the reading public. But he did, and these were in fact published the following year in a book called *The Garden of Asia*, a work of desperate sophistication, bearing every mark of its author's age and experience. It is intended to correct the 'ordinary Englishman' in his misassumptions about Japan, and is full of useful advice to this individual about how to arrange his house, instruct his servants, dress, eat and, above all, deal impressively with the Japanese shopkeeper: for example, by 'ignoring the garish lacquers and incrusted ivories with which the dealers besiege him, until at last they see that his taste is not to be led captive by rubbish'.

It is possible to read the book as an extended apologia for his expenditure in Japan; and so it may have been. But within this there is something very unusual: a chapter on the lives of Japanese women, analysing with clarity and sympathy how a policy of dividing women into wives and geishas ensured an equal but opposing enslavement for both. Where this strangely acute understanding originated cannot be known for certain, but as his gifts were critical and observant, not imaginative, it is likely that he saw in the Japanese state of affairs a formalised version of something he had noted with dread on his own behalf, in his own country: that women were either dull, in which case suitable as wives, or not dull, in which case not suitable. This matter obsessed him for the rest of his life, and he continued to view it as an impasse.

Even more than most writers, Farrer's tendency was always to write about himself, no matter what the ostensible subject. He would have had sympathy for anyone trapped, as Japanese women were, for he perceived this to be his own predicament. He arrived home on a Sunday night in the summer of 1903 to find, as travellers often do, that nothing had arrived, or gone away, in his absence. There were no welcoming festivities. 'The home-coming was momentous,' he wrote to Herbert:

It was Sunday. All the hotels were shut, all the trains rusting, the streets were full of shabby girls (such a shock after Japan) – I got lost, missed trains, fed on penny-in-the-slot machines till my last sou was gone, finally found myself at Skipton at ten o'clock at night with no obvious chance of getting on. Then I rose to the situation: I pawned my watch and chartered a special, and so home.

At home, his mother received him,

with commendable calm, and all the claws of the old
life closed on me – the East dropped away from me so
suddenly that it was almost tragic: at a blow it faded, and
the house and the place were just as they had always been
– till I felt in an hour I had never been away at all.

There was no enthusiasm for what he had learned
or seen in Japan. He wanted to tell everyone about
Japanese art and culture: about Hokusai, the Lady
Murasaki, or the wonders of the shrine of K'annon-
Sama. But his family, sensing that these were matters bearing only slightly upon the affairs of the
Ingleborough Estate, begged to be excused. 'Popular
interest in Japan seems to be bounded by raw fish and
paper houses,' he complained, 'My people are less interested than anybody.'

Indifference to Japan was not the whole of his problem. It was here that relations between Farrer and his
father and, to a lesser extent, with his beloved mother,
first began to deteriorate. There were financial reper-
cussions from the Japanese trip, the result of his prince-

ly way of living. James Anson Farrer kept his son on an allowance considered by the latter to be scandalously inadequate; no doubt he read of Reginald's magisterial shopping expeditions with qualified admiration. This, at any rate, was the first and last time that Reginald travelled in anything like the luxury he desired. From now on, his father kept him in view.

For the next ten years, this was the situation. His father's generosity didn't extend to a separate establishment, so he lived at Ingleborough and gardened – as we shall see – in the bits of land he could prise from the family, developing the Craven nursery into a respectable concern. He was made a J.P. and assisted with local liberal politics.

When he could, he got away: to London, to show plants and swell a few dinners at Downing Street, to the Alps in summer. At first, the surfaces were kept: the dressing gong, which could be heard all over the garden, obeyed, prayers mumbled, uncles and aunts of all kinds sat up with over endless games of whist. But he wrote to Herbert,

I am very badly bored indeed... a strained calm reigns

between me and my family. We really get on exceedingly ill, but we pretend that this is not so, and stolidly maintain the convention, with occasional lapses into candour. I was never built for the life domestic, and my whole soul is bilious with boredom. Home life has all the disadvantages of solitude, and none of its delights.

***

If anyone thinks of Farrer now, it is as a plant collector, a gardener, and a writer of garden books. But what he wanted for himself was to be a literary figure of grand repute – a playwright, a poet and a literary critic, but particularly a novelist. It is for this that he wanted acclaim, and it is impossible to understand his other achievements except in the light of this primary ambition. He was not alone, either, in fancying his prospects as a writer: in his own circle it was generally assumed he would write, and in undergraduate days Raymond Asquith had written daringly to him of:

> the ease with which a novelist could achieve immortality by simply putting the word 'fuck' into the mouth of one (or all) of the characters – I shan't do it yet, but I keep it

up my sleeve, if all other things fail. So please don't anticipate me.

Farrer did not in the event claim this distinction for his first novel, *The House of Shadows* (1906), an entirely mortal work written on the boat on the way home from Japan. It had some success: the anonymous critic for the *Times Literary Supplement* who thought well of it, praising the author as a writer to be remembered and the book as 'the novel of an idea', turned out to be Virginia Woolf, and this her highest compliment. And there were more – enough to raise expectations for his next one (*The Sundered Streams*).

'Oh Aubrey', he wrote as the novel progressed, 'I am getting so pleased about *The Sundered Streams*! I wonder if people are right, and there's something genuine in me somewhere?'

When the book came out, he sent it to Herbert. What the latter thought of *The Sundered Streams* was in fact a far from idle enquiry, for this is the book where those matters of unrequited love which always, for Farrer, had Herbert as their magnetic north, find their most lucid expression. In it, Kingston Darnley, a man married out of duty to a grim but suitable wife, meets a young woman – mannish, dishevelled in dress, unreserved in speech, who affects him strangely. She tells him they have been lovers through all eternity, and that their souls are destined to search for one another through an infinite number of lifetimes. Kingston realises this is true and that he loves her, but before they can run off together she dies in a fire, sacrificing her life to save that of Kingston's wife. He consoles himself with searching for her reincarnation on earth. He doesn't know that her reward for dying selflessly is release from the eternal bond that ties her soul to Kingston's, and so, when at last Kingston finds her reincarnated soul, it is inside a young man, and a young man, moreover, to whom Kingston means nothing. Kingston foresees his fate: he is condemned to batter for all eternity on a door that can never open.

Whatever one thinks of this as a plot, as a metaphor for the hopeless predicament of a homosexual man in love with a man who is not, it has, whether its author intended it or not, an admirable transparency; and it must raise the question of whether, for a man in that lonely position, going to sit at the end of the earth in a tent might be a matter of assuaging a greater pain with a lesser.

Farrer waited a long time for Herbert's reaction. At last came a note, written in haste. It was in keeping: 'You'll do better next time,' it said.

In fact, he had done better last time. *The Sundered Streams* was a critical and commercial disappointment. A sad diminuendo of praise accompanies Farrer's novelistic career, each book faring worse and regarded less than the last, until finally, with the dreadful *Through the Ivory Gate*, an embarrassed silence falls. Even his publisher, Edward Arnold, who probably published his fiction to secure the better business of his garden books, baulked at *Through the Ivory Gate*.

Unhappily for Farrer, the truth is that he was not a very good novelist. His plots are pointlessly complicated and constructed fitfully, as though he has already forgotten what he wrote on the page before. Moreover, his incurable solipsism – which elsewhere would be turned to good account – has the confusing effect of rendering all voices as his own, and, with one or two exceptions, makes no distinction possible between any of his characters, regardless of age or sex.

Whatever their failings as fiction, the novels cease to disappoint when viewed as biographical documents. All Farrer's books, including the garden writing and the travel books, can be read as open letters of complaint to his parents. But in his fiction (with the exception of his one historical novel, *The Anne-Queen's Chronicle*, in which the theme of the wife and the geisha is played out in the personal life of King Henry VIII) reproach festers openly. His novels are masterpieces of rancour. They typically feature scions of the provincial upper class, exceptional natures with exceptional needs, unmet and unappreciated by the ludicrous figures who control their destinies. Life at Ingleborough is portrayed unprocessed – down to the hair ornament his mother wore – with no attempt to make it sound attractive or to disguise character or place. Then, having established the models for his characters beyond the reach of human doubt, he makes them suffer horribly, and not from random fate, but as victims of their own social or moral principles. In one novel, a father develops a terrible disease – slow, terminal, hereditary and agonisingly painful – but, most unfortunately for him, he is denied the palliative of suicide by his inflexible Christian beliefs.

Against this background, more specific charges of neglect and ill-use parade: had, for example, anyone wondered what was the effect of educating young Reginald at home? They need only consult *The House of Shadows* for the answer:

> His was the usual fate of the child brought up in a perpetual jealous intimacy with a devoted parent – bliss and radiance through the earlier years, partial atrophy and bitterness for all the rest of his life.

James Anson Farrer and his wife responded to Reginald's novels by not reading them. It was their talent to ignore what they did not like and, he later said, to 'make a thing so by calling it so'. But in 1907 Reginald sailed to Ceylon, going part of the way with Aubrey Herbert, and there he did something that was much harder to ignore: he converted to Buddhism.

No one in our century, raised to admire multiculturalism, can really imagine the shame and affront that this produced amongst his family and even his friends. Outside the most rarefied academic circles, Buddhism itself was scarcely heard of in England. Indeed, for most educated men and women, if they had heard of it at all it was in the context of such people as Madame Blavatsky and her Theosophical Buddhist movement, with all its disturbing associations of spiritualism, occultism, freemasonry, spirit-rapping and the like. Osbert Sitwell describes the news of this latest development breaking upon the family to 'subdued polar shivering', and that after this his cousin's name was seldom invoked.

It could all perhaps have been better borne if Farrer had been discreet, but of course he was not. The travel book he wrote on his return (*In Old Ceylon*) is largely a rather excitable defence of Singhalese Buddhism, and from now on he incorporated – if that is the word for so imperfect an amalgamation – large slabs of Buddhist teaching into many of his books. At home in Ingleborough he achieved considerable local notoriety by wearing his 'Buddhist' robes (probably the Japanese court robes he bought in Tokyo) in public, and for giving lantern-slide shows to the village children thus attired. In point of fact, Farrer's Buddhist observances were highly selective and certainly never extended to abstention from alcohol; probably his real beliefs were nearer to the simple hope that, as he later wrote, 'Either all prayers and formulae have equal possibilities of validity, or none have any at all.'

But if the main reason behind his conversion was to annoy his family, as has been suggested, it worked. Sitwell tells how, after this, an 'indignant shudder passed through every gathering of relatives for prayer when... they besought the Lord that the Heathen might see the light.'

**

Farrer's position in his father's bad graces was now a permanency, but it was the making of him. It obliged him to earn money through garden books, a thing he might never have done with the benefit of a generous allowance. An undated letter to Aubrey Herbert shows he had misgivings about this sort of work, and aims to impress upon him that garden writing is not his true *métier*, but a necessary chore undertaken, as it were, with the left hand:

getting on towards the end of my garden book; it is turning out vastly longer than I had meant it to, and is the most utterly soulless, slave-driving drudgery. – Imagine writing something in which imagination plays no part: – the result is a sort of crushing deadness quite horrible to labour under.

One notes the apologetic tone: something about Aubrey Herbert always made Farrer feel small and uncertain, plucking at his sleeve for recognition. It is typical of his response to Herbert that he belittles his own area of brilliance before him, for garden writing, and gardening in general, *was* his true *métier*. He was prodigiously good at it. As a little boy he used to dissect flowers for his mother in the mornings, naming their parts to her as she dressed. By eight, he knew his botany book off by heart. Furthermore, all the things that made life hard for him – his circumstances and upbringing, his desires and expectations, his impossible egotistic personality – would, in the world of horticulture, be recast as virtues, and bring him to a place of greatness in its history.

Farrer's success as a gardener owes everything to the moment at which he entered it. At the start of the twentieth century, gardening was on the cusp of two great movements – the Victorian garden, in which the plant was the servant of the gardener, and the gardening of the twentieth century, still practised by most gardeners today, in which that relationship is reversed. It is a page of history crossed with contradictions and anachronisms and exceptions to its rules of progress, and re-crossed again, until it looks like an old maid's postcard. The following digression is a necessarily oversmooth account.

The three events that shaped Victorian gardening were these: developments in the manufacture of glazing bars; the abolition of tax on glass and bricks; and botanical exploration in South Africa and the Americas that introduced a new sort of plant, brilliantly coloured but tender. Horticulturally speaking, this made the nineteenth century the age of the glasshouse. On estates all over England great frames of wood and metal were raised, curvaceous as the Taj Mahal, and upholstered in acres of glass. They were ovens for flowers: inside them, the heat from furnaces that were never allowed to go out forced thousands of yellow calceolarias, blue lobelias, red pelargoniums and such into flower for the summer, when they would be planted outside in coloured patterns. Colour – and colour contrast – were the matters of interest: geometric designs were drawn out on the turf and contiguous segments of these crammed with plants in contrasting primaries, to make coloured spandrels and quatrefoils appear as though set into the ground; two-hundred-foot-long borders were planted up in rainbow stripes, with the minutely differing colours of flowers leaching prismatically into one another. This was the process called 'bedding out'. Were Victorian gardening to be described in two words, they would be those.

For obvious reasons, bedding out was gardening for the very rich, but there was a demotic twist to this, for the luminaries of the piece were not the nobles or plutocrats, but their head gardeners. The Victorian head gardener – Joseph Paxton is the most famous example – was a man of parts, being also architect, manager and landscape artist. And the annual production of these designs was an exercise to further his own prestige, although the prestige of the employer did not exactly suffer. It was said in the mid-century that a man could measure his wealth in his bedding list: ten thousand for a squire, twenty for a baronet, thirty for an earl, forty for a duke, and for Alfred de Rothschild, who wished to make his position clear, forty-one thousand.

In the bedding system, the plant itself was not important; it was merely a colour element in a scheme. Apart from the heat needed to make it bloom, its needs were not consulted. Its natural qualities – leaf, habit, shape of flower – were viewed not as an ornament but as a challenge to the levelling hand of the designer. The effect aimed at was as close as possible to enamel inlay, achieved in the winter by filling the beds with coloured sand and pebbles. By the end of the century the bedding art had refined itself into a practice called 'carpet bedding'. For this, dwarf plants were laid out in more elaborate devices, like garlands, ribbons and bows, monograms, or letters forming the names of proprietary brands. They were then clipped close to resemble the pile of a carpet – a most ingenious conceit, when one considers that carpets were originally devised as a way of bringing the garden indoors.

This was all to be blown away by the mighty bellows of one man, the gardener, writer and publisher William Robinson. Here was the patriarch of hardy plant gardening; that is to say, the kind we do now, using plants that grow naturally in our climate. Our borders are planted with hardy perennials, flowering shrubs are underplanted with bulbs that we encourage to 'naturalise' (Robinson's term) in our lawns. Robinson invented this, and in so doing created what we can now see as the horticultural lodge of the Arts and Crafts Movement, that arose in revolt from the broderied opulence of the mid-Victorian period. Ruskin influenced him, of course, and with that inspiration he started up a horticultural press, issuing from it thunderous denunciations of carpet bedding, and praise for the loveliness of plants garbed simply in their natural state.

Every innovation of Robinson and Gertrude Jekyll, his friend and ally in all of this, is just ordinary gardening to us now. From the perspective of our own century it is hard to imagine that none of this existed before, or how revolutionary these practices seemed at the time. To tighten the focus a little, an analogy may be drawn between the development of English gardening in the nineteenth century and that of English cookery in the twentieth. Bluntly put, there were two kinds of food at the start of that period: home cooking, absolutely plain, all innocent of foreign pretensions, and fancy cooking, produced by professional cooks in the houses of the rich. Then, some time after 1950, it all changed. The professional cook disappeared from private houses, and cook-hostesses would produce from their own kitchens a new kind of food: the regional dishes of France and the Mediterranean; neither plain nor fancy but fresh, simple, seasonal and acting not at all incidentally as an advertisement for the cultural sophistication of the cook. This closely follows the model of Victorian horticulture, where the two kinds of gardening, cottage gardening (plain) or bedding out (fancy), are then overturned by the introduction of hardy plant gardening (fresh, seasonal).

Elizabeth David figures conspicuously in the culinary model. She did not invent French or Italian provincial cooking, but through her books was largely responsible for its popularity. She was also a searing snob on matters of food who brought cookery writing into the area of literature and whose authority derived from extensive personal explorations in Western Europe. In the horticultural model, that figure is Reginald Farrer.

Farrer was an alpine, or rock gardener. To many in

the twenty-first century, this pursuit may not strike the mind as obviously analogous in style or anything else to the cookery of Elizabeth David, whose practices we associate with clarity, lightness and simplicity, and whose recipes seem to distil the sensual properties of the Mediterranean. Rock gardening, on the other hand, may call more domestic scenes to mind, in which the back walls of suburban gardens largely feature; or else those strange abandoned structures one still finds in public parks: cliffs of fake boulders dressed with elephant-grey cement, their crevices stuffed with lager cans. But a hundred years ago, the rock garden was a homage to nature and to the world's wildernesses. To the Edwardian eye, a limestone rockery planted up with alpine flowers would carry the refreshing connotation of a wild mountain landscape, and would confer, for reasons we will come to, a cosmopolitan distinction upon its owner, as being one who visited the Alps in summer and saw these tiny beauties for himself. When the Swiss botanist, Henri Correvon, visited the stupendous rockeries of Sir Frank Crisp at Henley, he reported approvingly that he 'found [himself] whistling an alpine tune'. That was the desired effect.

Alpine gardening might be described as an extreme branch of hardy plant gardening, and its history an extreme version of the history just related, for the first rock gardens, far from celebrating the natural beauty of plants, had no flowers at all. They were concerned with alpine scenery, not its flora, and they were follies for rich men. Immense rockworks were raised, often in imitation of actual mountain ranges. In the late 1830s an entire valley in Chamonix appeared at the end of Lady Broughton's garden in Cheshire, its realistic crests and ledges all sparkling with marble snow.

Farrer despised this sort of thing, as he did everything he considered 'Victorian', and assumed, not wholly correctly, that these mountains were bald because the Victorians couldn't grow alpine plants. They could, but not very well. And even by Farrer's day, when alpines were brought home from expeditions to collect hardy plants, most nurserymen found that they sickened and died, set no seed and were generally a bad bargain. Farrer, for reasons we are about to see, knew how to grow them, and under the influence of his writings the successful cultivation of a reluctant or finicky plant became the aim and purpose of alpine gardening, as it is today.

For the biographer, the real interest here is in the
social forces that operated upon hardy plant gardening,
and particularly alpine gardening. They push both up
and down in a way peculiarly suited to Farrer's own
circumstances, by minimising the importance of wealth
(hardy plants need no glasshouse and, in the case of
alpines, little land) and asserting that of taste, discern-
ment, culture and, crucially, of breeding as the only
begetter of these qualities. Farrer never stopped insist-
ing that alpine plants were no respecters of wealth.
His writings belong in that tradition of garden writing,
ancient in origin, condemning the horticultural pretensions of the rich. And yet by no means did he write
for the poor. He wrote for people like him: people in
possession, in Cyril Connolly's impeccable phrase, of
a private income and a classical education; people
who were supposed to read his novels, but didn't. The
gardening books are elaborate in syntax, dense with
abstruse literary and historical allusions, fluttering
with Latin tags and French motifs. They advert repeat-
edly to the impressive range of cultural experience in
the author's personal stock. A frilled begonia, for example, produces in him 'that *morne étonnement* which

Swift is said to inspire in the French mind'. *Primula auricula* is the particular shade of yellow 'which I last saw in the palanquin that was conveying the Empress Dowager to the railway station in Peking'. When he is deeply stirred, little bubbles of Greek burst on the surface of the page.

A central assumption of his books is that the garden's owner – his reader – is responsible for its aesthetic development. So it will come as no surprise that the person actually affected by all this was not Dives, the rich man, at all, but Dives' head gardener – the creative force of Victorian times, usually a brilliant man of humble stock, who now found his prestige bleeding into the veins of his employer, as he was steadily demoted to an artisanal role. But, as far as alpines were concerned, there was one hard fact at the bottom of this snobbery: Farrer discovered that the successful cultivation of these plants was a case of replicating their native conditions. To do that, you had to have seen the plant in its home. In 1906 only the leisured class holidayed in the Alps.

Farrer had seen plants in their homes. It was usual for families like his to travel to the mountains of Savoy and Austria. But most of his life had been spent on

Ingleborough, which is a limestone scar, and a natural rock garden. On his lonely walks as a boy he had seen the little saxifrages and anemones blowing on boulders where the scar had elbowed through the turf, and noted how the stones were set. He could instruct his readers in the laying of stones. But he had a more unusual advantage: he knew what went on inside mountains. Under the estate's crust ran the system of conduits and tunnels, beautiful with stalactites and stalagmitic pillars, known as the Clapham caves. This was a very popular tourist destination in the nineteenth century, particularly after Reginald's great-grandfather discovered that what had always been supposed the back of a shallow cave was in fact a mere membrane of stalactite, and this, when broken down, gave upon a cave that pushed a thousand yards into the hillside, ending in a deep black pool. There was a door in the hill, but the family had fitted it and they held the key. Often Reginald would take candles and a hammer and lead parties of house-guests deep into the mountain. He took Violet Asquith down there in 1911, when she was struck by the epigrammatic flourish of his conversation and, less kindly, by his resemblance to a troglodyte. However, it was here he saw the rains percolating through the shell of the mountain, and this enabled him to form his theories of perfect drainage and irrigation from *beneath*, which were entirely new and greatly enlarged the scope of what could be grown.

My Rock Garden was published in 1907. It was an immediate and lasting success. He followed it with *Alpines and Bog Plants* (1908), *In a Yorkshire Garden* (1909) and *The Rock Garden* (1912). Some time after 1910 he began work on the mighty *The English Rock Garden*, a two-volume encyclopaedia of alpine plants, which was not finished until 1915 and would not be published until after the First World War. These books changed garden-writing for good. Up until now, serious garden-writers delivered their advice in tones of omniscient authority, remote and unassailable. Farrer wrote as a personality, full of prejudice and indefensible opinions. He was a garden snob. Everything he admired was what we would call today 'good taste' in the garden; and he is at the head of that extensive tribe who made such matters as the choice of single over double flowers, of small narcissus over large, of blue flowers over orange, of scent over size, of species over garden cultivars, of simple petals over ruffled, of flat-headed chrysanthemums over globular, incurved varieties* into a means by which a refined sensibility might be advertised, or a coarse one betrayed. He had opinions on many matters, not by any means all of them to do with gardening. He digressed unchecked into subjects like the Savoyard royal family, the novels of Jane Austen (whom he worshipped), the wines of Bolzano, Elizabethan folklore, and where in Bond Street one could buy a good tie pin. But his greatest influence was in his writing style, which used the ornate conceits and devices of a 'high' literary style to describe plants and even humble garden procedures. Here he is on how to make soil:

> The ideal rock-garden mixture should be at once nutritious, light and spongy, not clogging in winter rains, nor yawning under summer suns, but always cool and friable and loose in the hand, like the consistency of a rich and perfect seed cake, crumbling yet unctuous to the touch.

*He described the large, globular chrysanthemum as 'a moulting mop dipped in stale lobster sauce'

Before Farrer, the colour of a plant might be described as 'a pleasing blue'. William Robinson, himself a man with some pretensions to a writing style, considered that 'fine evergreen foliage and handsome large flowers' dealt adequately with *Helleborus niger**. But not Farrer. He would have a certain aconite: 'in texture like Japanese silk-crepe, and of the oddest, most subtle and lovely colour, like oyster-coloured chiffon over a blue slip'; *Anemone robinsoniana* possessed a 'quakerish loveliness'. *Meconopsis punicea* at Chelsea droops 'like the flag of some London Club on a tired sad day of November'.

The contagion of his style can hardly be overestimated. Vita Sackville-West ranked him just below D. H. Lawrence as a 'writer on flowers', calling him half-poet, half-botanist, and admiring his extravagance as well as his accuracy; and well she might, since it was his example that gave her leave to carry on like this herself. And not just her: at the back of this book you will find a few examples of garden writing in the post-Farrer era, when, up until about 1950, it was literally impossible

*for Farrer's description of this plant, see p.97

to call a spade a spade. Here it is enough to say that it was he who, more than anyone, dragged garden writing into the area of *belles-lettres*: an impressive show of resourcefulness, as this was an enclosure to which his novels would not admit him.

Erudition was not all that was aired in his garden books. He also used them to pursue his grudges against his family. Descriptions of his own garden at Ingleborough dwelt with venomous indignation on the stinginess and ignorance of what he called 'The Family' or, with martial overtones, 'The Powers'. The rub was in the fact that Farrer's garden was not his, but his parents', and he had to take what he could get from them in the way of land and men to work it. He had to be his own gardener: an inestimable advantage to his work, as it happened, but not one he always appreciated.

The result was frustration and ill-feeling, a garden that rarely met his own standards, and struck even the unbiased observer as slightly disappointing. But he did achieve one unique effect with his cliff garden, admired in his time as 'the only truly natural rock garden in the country'. There is nothing left of this marvel now, though the lake at Ingleborough still reflects on its far bank the long, high cliff where it once flourished. This cliff, he wrote, was an ideal place for his experiment, 'riddled with deep cracks and crevices and fissures, the very place of all places that heart could desire'.

Immediately, he set about devising methods of seeding it, like lowering men down the cliff on rope ladders and, so it is said, rowing a small boat out into the middle of the lake and shooting at the cliff-face from a rifle loaded with seed. The results were gratifying; next year, the cliff broke into flower. It bloomed so heartily that Farrer thought he had established a self-sustaining colony of alpines, to speak for him in perpetuity. 'As for me', he wrote, 'the sight makes me say *Nunc dimittis*; so far and away more satisfactory is it than any other thing that I have yet achieved upon this sinful and ineffectual earth.' But in time they failed, and the cliff is empty now.

Farrer has one last gift to the language of gardening, and as it is the one good thing to come out of that blight on his temperament – the destructive egotism that a friend called 'the eternal "I"' – it is rather like the scrap of hope in the bottom of Pandora's box. To explain: Farrer was touchy, reproachful, extremely demanding, painfully solipsistic, disposed to view the rest of the world as a deficient source of comfort. This made him wretched most of the time, but it also allowed him to sympathise to an unusual degree with the exigent requirements of alpine plants. While alpines need no heat, little space and no extensive staffing arrangements, they do exact their price in personal attention. An alpine plant in cultivation in, say, Surrey, is a plant living *en prince*, a plant that is waited on hand and foot. It only likes an alpine climate – the drainage of high slopes, the security of a long winter settled under snow, the sharp punctual sunshine of an alpine summer – and unless a tolerable replication of its native conditions is provided, it will die. In England, where the climate is lightless, mild and damp – exactly what an alpine hates – it must, whether you grow it in a pot or in a rockery, be coaxed and fussed over with resourceful assiduity if it is even to *think* of flowering for you. Special programmes must be devised for individual plants, involving bespoke watering regimes and choice titbits in their soil; at the least whiff of adversity you must rush out in the night to suspend little panes of glass over their querulous green rosettes.

Farrer could grow these things because he was pre-pared to indulge their whims. He allowed his alpines to be insatiable, their dues no less than their desires. In his books a patience is preached, as limitless as anything proposed by Penelope Leach for a teething baby (*Primula spicata*, for example, 'a dream of beau-ty', must be 'sat up with night and day when in flower, that it may be prevailed upon, with food and flattery, to set seed'); and as for his cultivation techniques, he considered it a dereliction of care to put a plant in the ground without introducing the soil, with all tender-ness, to *each of its roots individually*.

Farrer identified with alpine plants. His recommen-dations for the treatment of plants were a prescription for his own usage, should anyone care to consult it. This is not fanciful. One cannot be long exposed to writings where plants get bored and lonely, and need company, and must, like witty but difficult house-guests, have not just food but, 'such succulent delights that they will thrive, and unfold, and sparkle for you afterwards', without detecting a second, unfloral presence here; nor read the following case for their cultivation without finding inside it the writer's own epitaph:

the enormous majority of alpine plants, despite the peculiarities of their natural conditions, are quite extraordinarily easy... dazzlingly brilliant and profuse in flower, cosy, compact and dwarf in shape; and they have... a personal force of attraction such as no other plant can hope to rival – the attraction of limitless courage, of their stubborn individuality, of their indomitable ingenuity against difficulty, far up in the grim and lonely places of the world.

This trait of Farrer's resulted in a new language for horticulture. For him, plants had temperaments: they are 'miffy' and 'sulking', 'fractious', 'repining', 'homesick', 'resentful', 'demanding' and 'capricious'; yet, when treated in accordance with their dues, they are transfigured: not grumpy now, but 'trustworthy', 'cheerful', 'generous', 'grateful' and 'lovable'. Nobody wrote like this about plants at the time. Now everybody does, quite as a matter of course: Farrer's temperament furnished a vocabulary so expressive and pertinent that it was universally adopted as the natural language of all gardening.

***

Who would look after him like this? Not Aubrey
Herbert, who in about 1910 received a letter concerning
his shortcomings in this regard. It is very long, and
reads as though written late in the day:

> I am swamped and put away on a shelf by the violent
> realisation of all your innumerable friendships, activities,
> manifestations in which I obviously have no share… you
> didn't give me what I wanted this time. You've prevented
> me for a long while to come, from coming to you for help
> and encouragement… I rather wonder at you. For you
> know how my nature works: and you have never done
> such a thing before: but now it'll take me a long time to
> uncoil to you again.

He signs off stiffly, but starts again at once, in
remorseful and pleading vein:

> At this point I don't care if I become abject and
> Elizabethan: here I am, approaching the staid and unemo-
> tional thirties, when all the heart's vacancies are supposed
> to be closed – and yet (as you very well know, damn you)
> at your call I would still come or go like a two-year-old:
> for the possibility of your approach, yours alone among

mortals, would I hike my aged bones out of bed after midnight: your voice has power to smooth my fur and retrench my claws in a manner nothing short of miraculous to the outer world – confound your confidence in all your little wheedling ways!

This must have given Herbert some idea of where he stood. But he was a busy man now, and all was well with him. Since the days at the Japanese embassy, his career had been one where worldly success is achieved with no corresponding expense of ideals. Nor had he ever stopped doing what he pleased: he had adventured most dashingly in the Balkans and was becoming a figure of some political influence in the cause of Albanian nationalism. In 1911 he came back briefly from Constantinople to stand as Conservative MP for his local town of Yeovil, and was promptly returned.

The contrast between this and his own restricted and compromised situation would not have been lost upon Farrer. The year before, he had tried to enter politics himself as a Liberal, with a thousand pounds given him by his father to cover his election expenses. He campaigned, on a free trade ticket, for the unsafe seat of

Ashford, in Kent, posting bills with the slogan, 'SEND FARRER HERE', written above a drawing of the Houses of Parliament.

This may have struck the electorate as insufficiently detailed; at any rate, it was Mr. Lawrence Hardy, for the Conservatives, who was returned. In truth, it was no real loss, except of face: he hadn't the disposition for party politics, being shocked by political expedience and bored by the obligations of electioneering, complaining of these to Herbert during his brief campaign:

> In the evening I went to preside at a Liberal concert. Oh bless us and save us, what a performance. It lasts, believe me, for five hours; and I expect I lost vastly in public esteem by only putting up with three.

It is said that he spent his father's thousand pounds on bulbs.

In 1911 Aubrey Herbert got married to Mary de Vesci, a girl who was no less than she should be in the way of looks, character and birth. The list of their wedding presents read like a pauper's delirium. Soon after this, Farrer went to stay with them at Pixton, their estate in the West Country, partly to advise the new Mrs Aubrey on the garden. Mary, perhaps as a result of prior exposure, was not much looking forward to it. She wrote to her mother,

> Really they [our guests] will be quite alright and restful with the possible exception of Mr. Farrer, who is I believe a malevolent gnome, with a wish to be fascinating but an ill restrained bitterness of tongue.

This was prescient: Reginald could not make the gestures of deference due to Mary as Aubrey's wife, or sustain for long the jovial supporting act that a new wife likes to see in her husband's old friends. Instead, he overwhelmed the occasion, monopolising Aubrey, dispensing Eastern wisdom early and late (failing signally with this to captivate Mary, who took to calling him 'Buddha' behind his back), and finally being extraordinarily rude to Aubrey's sister, Vera, in such a way that no one could overlook it.

'If her account is true', Mary complained, 'he really seems to have been poisonously insulting. It does make

me feel rather annoyed because, though one is sorry
for him, he has got the dwarfish ill-nature and canker
about him somewhere that is very irritating and
wounding.'

Mary tolerated Reginald somewhat better in the
garden, where he advised her conscientiously and
well on plants. He was by now becoming a considerable figure in the world of English gardening, and
his advice was much sought after, though he never
descended to professionalism. He was invited to join
the Horticultural Club, the eminent members of which
would meet for dinner at a London hotel to discuss
plants and gardening matters. He met and corre-
sponded with the directors of the Botanic Gardens at
Edinburgh and Kew, and other garden luminaries like
Ellen Wilmott, William Robinson, Canon Ellacombe
and George Bunyard, the celebrated pomologist –
dedicated committee men and women whose task it
was to conjoin the Victorian obsession with classifica-
tion to the Edwardian ones with rank and pedigree, and
bring their combined weight to bear upon the vegetable
world. They pinned medals on the breasts of pears,
and established the right of, say, a grape to call itself

'Muscat of Alexandria', or a garden crocus to bear its varietal name.

One of these was E.A. Bowles, perhaps the greatest gardener of his time. By 1910, when Farrer met him, Bowles was forty-five, though he bore himself as older, and had attracted most of the available distinctions in the world of horticulture. He was an exceptionally good and kind man, whose face in photographs shows the prematurely weazened features of an innocence that has been allowed to mature undisturbed. If, being unmarried, the unused tenderness of his heart flowed into good works for the benefit of young boys, this is a fact from which nothing remotely sinister should be inferred. He travelled to the Alps several times with Farrer on plant-collecting expeditions, and the sweetness of his character may be confirmed by his forbearance when Farrer lampooned his lack of climbing skills in the books (*Among the Hills* and *The Dolomites*) he wrote about these excursions.

Not everyone so treated – the list was long and included his unfortunate younger brother, Sidney, a squashed and silent individual – was as restrained: a certain Henry Clutton-Brock, whose vertigo Farrer mocked in print, loathed him vigorously for it. But Bowles took it all in good part. He had a true fondness and admiration for Farrer; so much so that when he came to write his own books he was happy to use them as promotional vehicles for his friend's ideas and career.

He asked Farrer to write the preface for the first of these, the best-selling *My Garden in Spring*, a work that shows how Farrer's influence was already operating upon the style of garden writing. It was a high distinction for the younger man, but the generous Bowles supplemented even this honour, extolling at length the 'master mind' of Farrer and his unique 'moraine' system of growing alpines. The passage begins, 'Then Arose the Prophet', and goes on to praise him in terms which must, even by Farrer's exacting standards, have seemed acceptable:

The abundant rainfall of Ingleborough and the local lime-stone, aided and abetted by river silt from the Lake's mouth and chips of all sizes from the mountain side, were only waiting for Mr. Farrer's master mind to plan their combination and lo! A new era dawned. The most discontented of his alpine treasures flourished, the great news went forth to the world, a series of books in slate-coloured covers became the foundation of all conversation, even at dinner, to the great annoyance of those who wait and therefore expect all things should come to them. This is a fact: a head gardener, in speaking of the extraordinary wave of the fashion of gardening, told me that the men in the house complained bitterly that, whereas once upon a time they picked up innumerable sporting tips and had much interesting gossip to listen to, nowadays the talk at dinner was all Latin names and about soils and gardening books. Now the moraine holds the field.

There was some truth in this: the rage for rock gardening grew to a great extent out of Farrer's books. But what it really shows is the thoughtfulness of Bowles, who had obviously noticed how his friend would like to shine in a wider world, and may have slightly overstated the case to please him. How Farrer rewarded him for this kindness, we shall soon see.

An impartial confirmation of Farrer's celebrity, and of the rising popularity of rock gardening, may be found in the fact that, in 1912 , he was asked to provide the leading essay for *The Horticultural Record*. This

Aubrey Herbert   Raymond Asquith

William Purdom disguised as a peasant for the expedition to
Kansu, 1914-1915, to gather seeds for *Dipelta floribunda*.

Sir Frank Crisp's garden at Friar Park, Henley-on-Thames,
with its 30-ft replica of the Matterhorn

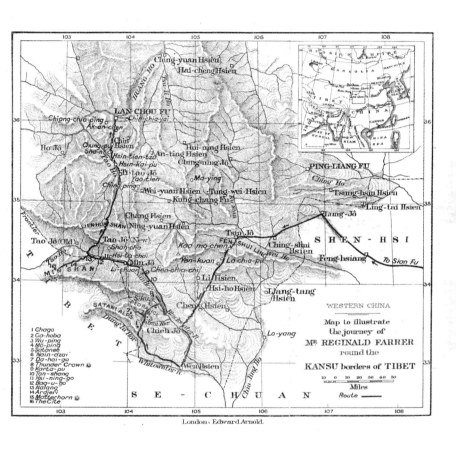

Map to illustrate Reginald Farrer's journey around the
Kansu borders of Tibet

Viburnum fragrans.

Viburnum fragrans (syn. *V. farreri*)

Cypripedium farreri
(watercolour painted by Farrer in China, 1914)

Gentiana farreri
(watercolour painted by Farrer in China, 1915)

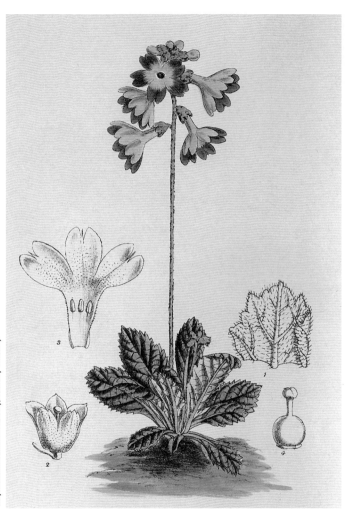

Primula spicata

379

Paeonia suffruticosa
(similar to the wild Moutan peony found by
Reginald Farrer in Kansu in April 1914)

stately book was produced to commemorate the International Horticultural Exhibition, the biggest horticultural show since 1866, and was intended to present an overview of the state of British horticulture. Farrer's essay – 'On Rock Gardens and Garden Design' – so impressed the reviewer for *The Gardener's Chronicle* that he declared himself 'stricken dumb with its effulgence'.

As for the exhibition itself, its intentions could hardly have been clearer if the words WEALTH, POWER, CONFIDENCE had been bedded out in calceolarias on a floral background of the Union Jack. This message issued from all corners. It was in the display of hothouse might put on by Leopold de Rothschild, who covered a quarter of an acre with hundreds of fruiting trees in pots, including twelve varieties of cherries, as well as (in May) figs, nectarines, peaches and grapes; it was more evident still in the exhibition of Chinese plants put on by the nurseryman James Veitch. The point was made that these were plants collected *in the wild* by Veitch's plant collector, Ernest Wilson; a point that would not have been lost on the public, who knew that China, closed for centuries to foreign trade, had been slowly prised open over the last few decades, mainly as a result of British initiatives. If Wilson had spent a decade poking around unobstructed in the Chinese hills, it showed how firmly the British toe was planted.

In the Japanese gardens section stood an object of interest to this narrative. A 'bronze Sacred Hoko bird', picked out by the reporter for *The Gardener's Chronicle* as an ornament of particular merit, had been bought by Sir Frank Crisp, a very rich lawyer with a baronetage of recent date and a garden at Friar Park, Henley-on-Thames.

His garden was famous for its extensive rockworks, modelled in imitation of alpine landscape, with caves below and peaks above, and having as their centrepiece a thirty-foot replica of the Matterhorn, made exactly to scale, and populated with humorous metal chamois. On this mountain more than two thousand alpine species were planted, using a method by which masses of a single plant were laid over the rocks, so that broad patches of intense colour would develop over the season. It was a method – and indeed a garden – highly commended by William Robinson, but scorned by Reginald Farrer as expensive and missing the point, which was, for him, to contemplate the singular beauty of the individual plant.

Now, when Farrer was asked by E. A. Bowles to write the preface to *My Garden in Spring*, he took the opportunity to air these opinions, clarifying his praise of Bowles' planting schemes with some illuminating points of contrast. For this purpose he singled out an anonymous rock garden:

> But what a display is here! You could do no better with coloured gravels. Neat, unbroken blanks of first one colour and then another, until the effect indeed is sumptuous and worthy of the taste that has combined such a garden... it is not a rock garden, though tin chamois peer never so frequent from its cliffs, bewildered with such a glare of expensive magnificence. This is, in fact, nothing but the carpet-bedding of our grandfathers...

It seems likely that Farrer, with his weakness for patricide of one form or another, had William Robinson in view when he wrote this. He had insulted him in print before now, and certainly the accusation of 'carpet-bedding' would annoy Robinson more than it would Sir

Frank Crisp. But Robinson's garden had no tin chamois in it, and Sir Frank Crisp's did.

Sir Frank's sense of humour was essentially pluto-cratic: his idea of a joke was to have his groundsmen pretend to fall into the lake and drown (a trick made possible by a quirk of landscape perspective) while he went on, apparently unperturbed, serving tea to his onlooking guests. When the book came out, in the spring of 1914, he didn't think this passage was at all funny. What happened now was the most scandalous thing ever to have troubled the serene surfaces of the gardening world. He published a retaliatory pamphlet, unambiguously entitled MR. E. A. BOWLES AND HIS GARDEN, attacking Bowles in the most unguarded terms, including barely veiled accusations of personal envy and malice. At once William Robinson agreed to print it, in entirety, in *Gardening Illustrated*. His friend, Ellen Willmott, the beautiful and accomplished gardener whose personality formed the rationale for the permanent exclusion of women from The Garden Society*, and was said by some to have been slighted in

*The still extant dining club for the gardening elite, where the owners of great gardens bring plants from their gardens and discuss them after dinner. Women may not be members.

love by the timorous Bowles, was loaded up with pamphlets and stationed by the gates of that year's Chelsea Flower Show, where she handed them out to Bowles' friends, and anyone else, as they came in.

Not one of these people seems to have noticed that Farrer, not Bowles, was to blame. Nor would it have done any good if they had. For Farrer had gone, with his debts of courtesy unpaid, away to north-west China to hunt for plants in the Himalayas.

***

It was the dream of his life to do this, and, in fulfilling it, he had no one to thank but himself. Looking at Farrer's career, one is impressed by its beautiful self-sufficiency. Through the popularity of his gardening books and the consequent rise in the popularity of rock gardening, he had himself contributed to the increased demand for hardy plants, and it was this that enabled him, at last, to do what he thought he may never, and lead a plant-hunting expedition to China.

Even so, it was not easy to arrange. He needed all his tenacity about him to get financial backing. At first, he

wrote to Sir Isaac Bayley-Balfour, director of the Royal
Botanic Gardens, Edinburgh, for his opinion of an
expedition to Yunnan. Might he also, he enquired further, get him some government funding for this trip – he
required £2,000 – on grounds of the great benefits it
would bring to the British botanic gardens? He might
not. Farrer's request seems to have produced some shud-
derings when it fell on the desks of his potential benefi-
ciaries. From Kew, Sir David Prain wrote to Bayley-
Balfour that they should on no account give money to
an amateur like Farrer, as this would set a most dangerous precedent, all comparable expeditions being funded
by 'private enterprise'. When Bayley-Balfour forwarded
this decision to Farrer, it was a minor discouragement
by comparison with his letter's main purport, which
was to stop Farrer from going to Yunnan at all. If he
must go, than he should go north, it said, to the untried
ground of Kansu. Yunnan, he wrote, was being system-
atically harvested by two other English plant hunters,
Frank Kingdon-Ward and George Forrest, and the latter
had just taken on a hundred native collectors for his
second year's work. Farrer was hoping for two.

Forrest and Kingdon-Ward were employees of what

Prain referred to as 'private enterprise'; in other words, the nursery trade, which had now replaced the botanic gardens as the main source of new plants into Britain. These nurseries traded in novelty, and it was a risky business: Veitch had sent Ernest Wilson 10,000 miles to fetch *Meconopsis integrifolia*, only to find it growing in another man's nursery. Such losses were borne with a bad grace, and a collector was expected to gain territorial hold over a known hill or valley, keeping rivals out until he had finished with it. This was understood by everyone, including the directors of the Botanic Gardens, which, though they no longer funded expeditions, maintained good terms with the nurseries to the benefit of each – a thought which may have occurred to Sir David Prain when considering the case of Farrer in Yunnan.

The Botanic directors must also have noticed that Farrer did not seem physically strong enough to be leader of such an expedition. In fact, he was tough: Clarence Elliott, who walked in the Alps with him, said he could climb for thirteen hours without tiring. But he did not seem so, and the life of a professional plant-collector was one of extreme hardship and loneliness in return for low pay and shabby treatment. Often they died of disease or murder. Their paymasters – both the men of commerce and the civil servants – were martinets, and in the safety and importance of their offices they allowed their imaginations to fail them when it came to the difficulties a man might encounter in these savage places. Correspondence between plant collectors and their bosses at this time is a history of grievance on the one hand and obduracy on the other. It was no job for a man of letters, as Farrer was widely perceived to be.

In the end, he did as he was told and went for two seasons to Kansu, quickly persuading himself that this was a destination far superior to Yunnan or Szechuan, as likely to yield plants of greater hardiness. He got no money from the government but set up a syndicate, selling shares in his plant haul, at a hundred pounds each, to garden-owners who liked to show their friends something rare and unavailable in commerce. Fortunately for him, his patrons could not, even now in 1913, imagine that by the time the seeds came back they would be putting their gardens to potatoes.

In the spring of 1914, having reduced his own

belongings to 'the materials of washing and the novels of Jane Austen', he set out overland, first class, to Peking. Some weeks before, on Farrer's instructions, another gardener, exactly Farrer's age of thirty-four, had taken the same journey on a third-class ticket. His name was William Purdom, and he was handsome. Photographs show the strong, thrusting features celebrated in totalitarian statuary, but marred by an expression of retreat.

Purdom was the son of a Northumberland gardener, and exactly the sort of gifted man whom Farrer's influence had done much to demote. In the old days, a gardener with his span of capabilities might have taken on the charge of some great garden, with all the independence and prestige conferred by that. As it was, Kew trained him, and sacked him unfairly, and after that he went to work as a plant collector, working four quite unappreciated seasons out in Kansu for the nurseryman, Veitch, and Harvard University. Back in England, it seems, none of the available positions appealed. One of the few known incidents of his life is his involvement in a strike at Kew – perhaps he had begun to regard his remote, insistent seniors, as, later, the troops on the

Western Front would come to feel about theirs. In any case, rather than go back as a drudge, he was now prepared to accompany Farrer, a virtual stranger, to Kansu, to be his guide and companion, his translator, to make everything in readiness for him wherever he went, and all for no pay except his personal expenses; and these, as we have seen, were far from princely.

It is impossible to overpraise this remarkable man or exaggerate what good fortune befell Farrer on the day he enlisted his help. After four seasons in Kansu, it was the least of his service that he knew the country and its flora, spoke the language and was very well-liked by the Chinese. The only large-scale maps of the region in existence had been drawn up by him on his previous journeys; he had fought with brigands, killing four; he had learned doctoring and photography. All the photographs that are later credited by omission, and sometimes directly, to Farrer, Purdom took. In fact, – and here was the fulcrum of their relationship – he took no credit for anything, deferring to Farrer in all matters of precedence, whether it was the making of important decisions or sleeping in the best bed. Farrer loved him and depended entirely upon him. What Purdom thought of Farrer, or any of it, we shall never know, as no letters of his from this time exist, and the whole account of their journey is from Farrer's side, largely in the two books he wrote about their two seasons in China. The first of these, *On the Eaves of the World*, is his most charming book: heartless, funny, self-delighted. It describes the happiest year of his life.

The province where Farrer and Purdom were headed, Kansu, lies slantways in the far north-west of China, its western edge bordering with Tibet. They were trying to reach its south-western extremity, where the map, wrote Farrer, became:

> almost wholly innocent of names, so smooth and bald of appearance that one can hardly believe it to be a tempestuous sea of mountain ranges. This region is neither Tibet nor China... it is the Tibetan territory of Amdor, a wild land of wild peoples, unvisited by travellers of less calibre than Potanin and Przewalski.

Potanin and Przewalski had led, in the name of botany, semi-military expeditions out of Russia in the 1870s and 1880s. It is safe to assume the invocation of their names is intended for Forrest and Kingdon-Ward, whom we are now to see as exemplifying that lesser calibre of traveller, content with what Farrer, debarred from them, now calls 'the warmer southerly latitudes' of Yunnan and Szechuan. Such tendencies in Farrer's writing, and his weakness for exaggeration, naturally raise the question of how dangerous a place this Amdor really was. Yet it seems that, for once, he has turned his telescope the other way, and the account he gives in *On the Eaves of the World* is inclined, if anything, to minimise the dangers. We know this because someone else was going to the same place, at the same time, on the same business as Farrer and Purdom. He was an American plant-collector called Frank Meyer, sent out to look for cherries and persimmons in Kansu by the U.S. Department of Agriculture.

Meyer was not a man given to exaggeration. The plainness of his speech amounted to homeliness. But he didn't like the sound of Kansu; he wished to be excused. From Peking he wrote a series of letters to his head of department, Mr. Fairchild, each one more tremulous than the last:

Kansu is a very interesting land but – very wild, also; there are tremendous regions that haven't been mapped out yet; there are quite some robber bands in existence, and I was advised to be careful as there are some bad fellows in these lands who haven't got the respect for a white man like the Eastern Chinese robbers have... Both Mr. Williams* and Mr. Peck, first secretary of the Legation here, considered it inadvisable for me to proceed into Honan, Shensi and Kansu for the present... The whole of the Honan province is now being terrorised by powerful bands of brigands; one of the high officials of the government was captured by these robbers only a few miles away from the city of Honanfu and they asked a big ransom before setting him again at liberty... Mr. Grant, a Britisher, was murdered with his three Chinese servants and companions some 5 or 6 weeks ago by some wandering Mongols, only a day or two out of Kaglan and he was an 'old hand' in China and certainly was not of a rash or haughty disposition.

The 'powerful bands of brigands' he speaks of probably referred to the operations of the bandit Pai Lang, known commonly as 'White Wolf', which, in 1913 and 1914, were on a scale sufficient to make him a regular

*An official at the American Legation

item in the London *Times*. To the delight of that pro-imperial publication, the Wolf and his robber army continued for many months to embarrass the new Chinese President, Yuan Shih-K'ai, who, despite the intervention of the minister of war and the deployment of hundreds of thousands of soldiers, consistently failed to suppress him. In the spring and summer of 1914, White Wolf travelled west through Honan and Shensi, sacking several large towns, murdering, burning and raping, until at last he came unstuck in Kansu. It was exactly the route taken by Farrer and Purdom (and the hapless Meyer). For much of their journey they rode just a few days ahead of the bandit army, through nervy villages prickling with rumour, where every official, bound by law to safeguard the lives of 'highly passport foreigner', would then do everything he could to stop them from getting out again.

Farrer and Purdom's retinue consisted of themselves, a few bearers, three servants and two ponies. (One of these, Spotted Fat, 'a pot-bellied little porpoise all covered, on a ground of creamy white, with what looked like countless splashes of tar in various degrees of fresh black intensity', was a horse of bad character, being both jittery and slothful, and would later jump off a plank bridge high over the Tao river, with Farrer still on his back). Behind them, a train of mules and carts carried their belongings and enough money for two years, in boat-shaped silver ingots. Farrer was delighted by it all: by the north Chinese inns which he found 'sweet and wholesome', by the heated clay platforms, called *kangs*, on which he slept, by the humorous peculiarities of his staff, the remoteness of the place and, above all, by the wondrous, comically majestic spectacle of himself, in the midst of his own expedition, borne up into the hills on a palanquin with *Northanger Abbey* open on his lap. He was always conscious of the figure he cut, and here, amongst people who had never seen a white-skinned man, he was something to look at. In one village he proved such a popular attraction that, unable to resist the opportunity for wit, he succumbed altogether and set himself up as a *tableau vivant*:

> The whole population... came raging through the court in a dense stream until one felt like Mr. Gladstone or Queen Victoria lying in state. At last, to give them full value for their trouble, we unfurled the big green tent in the central

hall of our apartment, and sat there posed before the mob on the lines of a realistic group at Madame Tussaud's representing renowned travellers in their tent.

***

It took a long time to get up to the plants. Much of northern China is made of a fertile, ochre-coloured clay, called 'loess', which stains the yellow river and grows nothing of horticultural interest. But a month after leaving Peking, they entered Kansu province and now, as they mounted on to the uplands of Kansu, described by Farrer as 'like glorified Lewes Downs', they began to see flowering shrubs like daphnes and lilacs, wild fruit trees in flower and a red birch (*B. bhojpattra*) with a domed head like a sycamore.

On 16 April, they found the flowering shrub *Viburnum fragrans* (syn. *V. farreri*). This slow-burning beauty 'whose blushing stars glister as if built of crystals' and last from December to March, is now the indispensable winter ornament of every garden in Britain. It had been found the year before (by Purdom) in Chinese gardens, but never as a wild plant. With it began a time of luck: the same foothills turned up a new buddleia, (*B. farreri*), grey-leaved, ample-flowered, with 'a delicious keen scent of raspberry ice', and pale-pink *Dipelta elegans*, 'with a reticulation on the lower lip of what seemed like orange velvet', and a yellow-flowered shrub like a daphne that lasted in captivity just long enough to be found a new genus and called *Farreria*.

On 18 April, Farrer lay resting on the hillside when he saw, as he wrote, 'certain white objects farther along the hillside, that were clearly too big to be flowers'. They were flowers, of course: he had found the white form of the Moutan tree peony, a shrub cultivated in China for thousands of years, and its flowers bred into scores of forms and shades, but consistently elusive as a wild plant. The beauty of its flower is impossible to exaggerate, though Farrer did his best with a passage, now quite famous, that ends with him in a state of physical prostration – his habitual posture when admiring a plant – in front of it:

...Here in the brushwood it grew up tall and slender and

straight, in two or three unbranching shoots, each one of which carried at the top, elegantly balancing, that single enormous blossom, waved and crimped into the boldest grace of line, of absolutely pure white, with featherings of deepest maroon radiating at the base of the petals from the boss of golden fluff at the flower's heart. Above the sere and thorny scrub the snowy beauties poise and hover, and the breath of them went out upon the twilight as sweet as any rose. For a long time I remained in worship, and returned downwards... to find that Purdom's only other record from his higher ascent was spiteful and hunch *ilex pernyi*.

The day belonged to him. But not the plant: that is named for Joseph Rock, as *Paeonia rockii*, after seed sent back by him in 1926 was successfully germinated. However, it was not collected from wild plants, like the ones Farrer saw, but from shrubs growing in a lamasery garden, and the resulting plants are viewed with suspicion by some modern botanists, who think they may be garden hybrids. Whether the shrub Farrer worshipped has ever been cultivated outside China is a point of botanical contention to this day.

***

Farrer and Purdom were not really looking for shrubs, but for alpines. In the Himalayan ranges, alpines occur at far higher altitudes than in the mountains of Europe. They had to go up. In early May their party turned west and crossed over the march into Tibet, with the aim of reaching a village called Chago – a tiny, ill-favoured place, known to be bellicose, but endowed with two prominent limestone mountains, in the cleft of which it sat. They were lucky to have left the southward path where they did, at the foot of Kansu, because White Wolf came down that road behind them with his army in spate, and made charcoal of those villages that Farrer had admired for their swept and pleasant inns and rosy-brown children. But another chance to be murdered soon came along, just after their arrival at the monastery of Chago.

The reasons behind this episode are too various and complex for the scope of this book. They derive from the type of Buddhism practised locally on the Tibetan marches, which over time had incorporated elements of Hinduism and the pre-existing religions of the place, and had become a pantheistic, polytheistic religion, populating the Tibetan skies with hundreds of temperamental minor deities. These gods had charge between them of all aspects of human fortune and endeavour, and jealously supervised conspicuous natural features, like lakes and mountains. Being spirits of the sky, they were thickly assembled in the higher mountain passes. To what extent these superstitions were shared by the monks of the yellow church, as the official Buddhist sect was known, is not clear.

Farrer took the view, common to English travellers in the nineteenth and early twentieth century – and very partial – that this was an 'impure' Buddhism, and that the 'Lamas' as the monks were wrongly called, exploited local superstition to maintain their political and economic hold over an area bulging with subterraneous gold, even to the point of endorsing murderous forays. This opinion colours his overview of events, but it takes no account of the justifiable fear of the monks for the safety of their religion were it to fall under the control of one of the foreign powers, like Britain, that had been sniffing round Tibet in the preceding decades.

Arriving at Chago in the time of the crops, Farrer

and Purdom went immediately into the hills to look for plants, splitting up to cover more ground. Purdom set off up a very steep and crumbly track, but Farrer saw there was a far more commodious path, if he only pushed away the pile of brushwood lying across it. This naturally turned out to be a sacred road and its use a severe transgression of holy rites, certain to cause crop failure; excuse enough for the priests, in Farrer's account, to incite the peasantry to come and murder them that very night. The murder party, who seem at this point to lack determination, failed to get in and kill them quietly in the night; but the next day, when Purdom, still unsuspecting, went out for a walk without his revolver, the male population of the village surrounded him, 'with arquebuses at rest and fuses lit, with the obvious intention of shooting him then and there'.

Instinctively diplomatic, Purdom did the right and calming thing. 'Armed only, then, with his fascinating smile', was how Farrer described him, 'and with hands thrown wide to show his harmlessness', he walked through the guns. Seeing this, other villagers who had come out to watch now began to argue his case, and Purdom, letting them, saying nothing on his own behalf, 'with unhastening step and deliberate pantomime of pipe-lighting, proceeded indifferently homeward, and arrived unscathed'.

For the next few days, as they made excursions up the mountain and down into nearby villages to investigate other bases for the summer, a nervous peace was kept. But then the weather turned to rain and hail, the mountain disappeared into the cloud; Farrer noticed 'a bustle of religious activity' now ensuing, with the whole population taken up into the hills by the senior cleric he called 'Abbott squinteyes' – an individual characterised also as libidinous and drunk – to pray in the sacred groves. That night, his Ma-fu or servant, who had run back over the pass in the dark and the rain all the way from the far village, woke him to say that 'the whole rage of this district was directed against ourselves, and against our own immediate peril had all those prayers and exorcisms been perpetrated', or words more immediately to that effect. The reason given was the hailstorms, held locally to be the result of Farrer and Purdom's presence on the holy mountain. They had torn up the young corn. The Chagolese had now issued instructions all down the valley for the villages and monasteries to go in party with them and kill the foreigners once and for all.

Farrer's group comprised seven people, if you included the small boy who had come across the pass with the Ma-fu, and they had five weapons, one of which was a swordstick. One wonders why the Chagolese found it necessary to amass such a force against them. Yet apparently they had, and this initiative must have perturbed Farrer much more than he later allows in print. He would have known what bellicose Tibetans could do. A few years before, the plant collector George Forrest had been attacked under similar circumstances at a Catholic mission station on the Yunnan-Tibet border by what he calls 'yellow Lamas' (they were probably not monks but angry locals). Forrest got away but the Tibetans caught two French missionaries, Pères Bourdonnec and Dubernard. Forrest later wrote an account of the massacre for *The Gardener's Chronicle*, which Farrer would certainly have read, and might at this moment have recalled how the printable things that were done to Père Dubernard in the days before his death included the extraction of his tongue and his eyes. Farrer and his group sat up all night with their four guns, with their plants and their silver in boxes behind them, waiting for the enemy.

Nobody came. In the morning, as the mules were being prepared for a prompt evacuation back into China, Farrer failed to provoke the slightest hostility when he crept conspicuously out to collect some primulas he feared he might not see elsewhere. After this, security dogged them: at the small walled town of Siku in South Kansu, they were briefly gated when raiders from over the border besieged the town, but the government, acting with surprising despatch, sent troops to clear the area, and Farrer and Purdom were loosed into the mountains behind Siku. Fortunately for them, these mountains – which Farrer, with his noted disregard for the Wade-Giles system of Chinese pro-nunciation, identifies by the names 'Thundercrown' and 'Rotderspitze' – stocked new plants just as good as the ones at Chago. On one mountain alone they found seven primulas, five androsaces and five poppies, all new, among them the tiny purple *Meconopsis lepida*, 'like little catherine-wheels woven from the purple prisms of the rainbow', as he put it. Like many of his generation, he was not embarrassed by fairies.

Farrer spent the summer of 1914 here, and north of here, in a range of mountains called the Min-Shan, collecting plants and formulating his opinions on such matters as Protestant border missionaries (against) and the practice of foot-binding (for) in such a way as to cause general annoyance when his book, with its generous perorations on these subjects, was published.

Plant-collecting is arduous and exacting work, the least part of which, as it has been said, is the finding of the plants. They must then be gathered in quantity and all plant material carefully dried and pressed between pieces of paper – sometimes in places where no paper may be found – to the standards of adhesive precision expected by the botanic gardens. Every plant requires detailed field notes to be written by hand. All must be done punctually and on the spot. At the end of the season, there is seed to be got, and for this the collector must retrace in two weeks what he first took months to cover, and must then find the plant he saw back in May, uneaten and still in health in October, with its seed already set but not yet dispersed – a catalogue of imperatives so hard to discharge that Farrer described it as 'the most harrowing form of gambling as yet invented by humanity', and declared that a shilling packet of seed would be cheap at sixty. A collector like Forrest would now send out his hundred men to strip the mountains of anything that rattled. But, despite being only two men and a couple of unskilled Chinese helpers, Farrer's party collected seed that was beautifully viable, so that even the ungracious Bayley-Balfour admired its vigour, saying it was the finest he had ever had.

***

In November it began to snow, and they went down to Lanchow to pass the slow winter. This is now a city of two and a half million inhabitants, the clogged capital of the poorest state in China, a place of bad building and worse air. But one cannot read Farrer's description of Lanchow, as it was in the winter of 1914, without wanting to go there at once for a holiday. He wrote of 'the vast and pure serenity' of the north Asian winter, 'its flawless light, its colour, its feeling, its atmosphere. There is hardly a day when it is not like champagne to take the air in Lanchow,' he wrote. It was a view much at variance with that of Frank Meyer, who had also made it through the season and was now wintering in Lanchow:

> Conditions are so primitive here in Lanchowfu as to be almost unbearable; hot water is not for sale, there are no decent eating houses; heating of rooms is done by open charcoal fires, with bad head-aches as results! And yellow river water is carried about in wooden buckets from the river to the houses and – horrible to say – in these very same buckets all the waste water is being carried again to the river and thrown out wherever the coolies see fit to do it. My assistant and I have both been unwell several times, we whites cannot and we will not get accustomed to such miserable ways of living.

He also wrote that Farrer and Purdom were in the city, adding mysteriously, 'these last two, however, are somewhat out of order and do not seem to be inclined to tell a fellow much.'

They would not have socialised much. They had met before, at Siku, where Meyer had arrived in some distress. His interpreter had struck at going any further up-country than this, and Meyer, speaking no Chinese, was brought, in his annoyance, to deal intemperately with this man in the hearing of Farrer's servants, and push him down the stairs. This was a mistake that poisoned his reputation for ever. Farrer, who also spoke no Chinese and was wholly reliant on Purdom's interpretative offices, could nevertheless see that here was someone faring worse than himself in comparable circumstances. He was not one to miss such an opportunity: what little is now known of Meyer's personality derives from the gleeful account Farrer wrote of this incident, wherein emphasis upon Meyer's incompetence, peevishness and dislike of the Chinese people allows many instructive points of contrast to be drawn with the Farrer expedition:

'I will stay here', he [the servant] consolingly said to his employer, 'and take home your body when it is recovered.'

This programme by no means appealed to Mr. Meyer, who had engaged this gentleman, not as an undertaker, but as an interpreter absolutely essential to his own ignorance of Chinese and Yamun ceremonial.

Meyer did in fact die in China, but not this time. He disappeared off the back of a steamer on the Yangtze river and was drowned one night in 1917, the same year as this episode appeared in *On the Eaves of the World*. He was depressive; doubtless this influenced his descriptions of Lanchow city just as Farrer's exuberance of spirits informed his own reports. Farrer had had a good season; sent back plants which, if not as numerous as the haul of, say, Ernest Wilson, were of great garden value, for he was not interested in novelty but beauty, and all his things were ravishing.

Farrer spent that winter sitting up in Lanchow, writing to Yuan Shih-K'ai, the President of China, with his views about the state of affairs on the border, and shopping. So ruinous were his expeditions after trinkets that his Ma-fu, after begging him vainly to desist, took to chaperoning him on walks. Even Purdom was sent down the frozen valley after a pair of antique copper vats that Farrer had coveted on their way up. He dispatched this piece of business masterfully, without bothering Farrer with worries and details; exactly as he dealt, to Farrer's slowly unfolding relief and gratitude, with every task he was set on this two years' trip. From Lanchow, Farrer wrote Bayley-Balfour a letter of purest good intention, requesting that some of their best finds might be named after Purdom, and asking him if he could help find Purdom a senior post in a public garden. His terms of commendation are notable:

> A year's experience gives me only an ever-increasing admiration for my fellow-worker, whose keenness, resourcefulness and indefatigable endurance after plants are like nothing I have ever imagined... I feel to owe him a personal debt almost embarrassing in extent: for he is doing all this now, without one halfpenny of gain, for pure love of the thing, without hope of even any kudos except what I condescend to allow him! [Furthermore]... there is my own personal admiration and gratitude to the man, & my personal regard for him... it is he, after all, who makes the expedition possible: without my being supposed to know it, *he looks after me as if I were a hybrid of P. calliantha X P. spicata.*

The italics are mine, but the sentiment could only be Reginald Farrer's. The entry for *Primula spicata* in *The English Rock Garden* we have already seen.*

It would have been fresh to his mind, for his chief work of that winter in Lanchow was correcting the

*page 55

proofs of this enormous work, begun some years
before. The idea of doing this entirely from memory, in
a place without libraries or any botanical resources
whatsoever, may appear ill-advised, but to him it was
a source of pride and happiness to have such a capa-
cious memory. He would rather do it this way and
meet charges of inaccuracy by reminding the reader of
the circumstances of the undertaking. The surprising
thing is how few inaccuracies there are in a book of
two large volumes containing about 10,000 entries.
His aim in compiling it was to make a comprehensive
encyclopaedia, in English, of all the alpine plants
known at that time to botanic science; to name them
correctly, identifying and discarding all synonyms, and
to describe each plant and its cultivation. To achieve
this, he had to comb through every available authority
on the flora of each country, to pick out the alpines,
translate their botanical Latin into botanical English
and then to render the resulting mysteries ('an aucules-
cent herb of circinate vernation with the leaves impar-
ipinnatipartite or uncinate-lyrate, with mucronate-
crenulate lobules' is the example he gives) into readable
English.

The English Rock Garden is remarkable as a feat of taxonomy, and for the testimony it makes to Farrer's personal experience of alpines, almost inconceivable in scope for a man of thirty-four. But it is also a masterpiece of translation, an early dictionary, that puts into the vernacular what has been protected for the use of a few by the language of scholarship; and it has some of the marks of such works: the consuming intellectual energy, the taking of liberties, the generosity with conclusion and opinion. The taxonomy is precise; the definitions loose, to say the least. A very few examples must do:

Primula secundiflora: the outside of the bell is of a waxen dulled flesh-colour, filmed with a strange powdery bloom, and suffused with lines and nerves and flushings of claret and deep rose, with blue mysteriously suggested over the whole, omnipresent as the faintest of tints, like a whiff of onion in a good salad.

Phyteuma (sp): What this race has done to be called especially The Plant or The Vegetable Growth, beyond all other plants and vegetable growths, is not to be known by man.

Helleborus niger: so called because its heart, or root, is black, while its face shines with a blazing white innocence unknown amongst the pure of heart.

Primula marginata:... varies copiously, and the gardener had best go and choose his forms. He is particularly recommended to go to the valley of La Maddalena, above San Dolmazzo de Tenda, not only because *P. marginata* exists there in the most rampant profusion... but also because that valley is further occupied by a famous English botanist, one Mr. Bicknell, who there has a house, and spends long summers, in the course of which he asks nothing better than to show the treasures of the hills to all such fellow-collectors as desire to see them. Therefore, in asking him for guidance the gardener will not only be gaining profit, but giving pleasure also – a holy and pleasing thought.*

***

The second season in Kansu disappointed the expectations raised by the first. The range of mountains they

---

*The Rev. Clarence Bicknell detested other plant collectors in his valley, and had once repelled Farrer when he had tried to visit him there.

covered turned out to be granitic, not calcareous, and confirmed Farrer's Ingleborough-grown distrust for granite, as yielding a sparse and monotonous flora. It is true that he found his single best plant this year: a light blue gentian, possessing, he wrote, 'a shattering acuteness of colour: it is like a clear sky soon after sunrise, shrill and translucent, as if it had a light inside.' This was the plant that arrived at Edinburgh bearing the label *FARRERI* and so identifying itself to Bayley-Balfour as the plant that Farrer most particularly wanted to bear his own name. But the expedition was not saved. The book that he wrote about it, *The Rainbow Bridge*, is distinguished by sadness, but probably less for the sake of the plants they failed to find than for the fact that it was written in England, two years into the Great War.

Farrer knew about the war in the winter of 1914, but he experienced its scale and meaning only through letters and old newspapers, and from the sudden intensification of religious activity amongst the Buddhist monks, who set themselves to work for peace with long, insistent chantings and prayers and urgent ringings of bells. It was this noise that first alerted Farrer to the gravity of the situation in Europe. The war had not touched him then. But back in London in 1917, when he had been to the battlefields of Ypres, and many of his friends were dead, he understood something about world war that was given to much greater writers than him to define: that they are acts of collective forgetting, and make the old world irrecoverable. Threatened with that oblivion, memory becomes precious. Farrer saw this. Remembering a day at the end of that Tibetan summer of 1915, when 'happiness flooded into me like wine into a cup', he wrote: 'Foreign travel, O reader, has its very real advantages, and all the pleasant scenes you have collected are so many medicine bottles stored on your shelves against the maladies of life.'

In 1916, when Farrer returned, the maladies of life in England had made the world of horticulture unrecognisable. That April there was only six weeks' supply of grain on the island; every piece of ground was given to vegetable production, and the horticultural press ran articles about whether the fruits of berberis and viburnum were edible. The dampening effect of this on the market for rare alpine novelties can easily be imagined. Farrer's own nursery had gone bust at the beginning of the war, and he had had to bail himself out by selling seed from his Kansu expedition, at an insulting price, to a Liverpool cotton-broker called A.K. Bulley who ran a successful seed nursery. Now Bulley was giving his seeds away. In the Botanic Gardens at Kew and Edinburgh, the men had gone to war. By 1917, Bayley-Balfour would complain that, 'I have not a man looking after my plants who would have been allowed to come near them in the old days.' Most of Farrer's plants died of neglect.

William Purdom stayed in China, working for the Chinese forestry department. The horrible life that he went to, of boredom and solitude, living in a rail-car on the Kin Han Han railway, gives the measure of how little he cared to return, or to enlist. Most of Farrer's friends – that dutiless generation – had thrown themselves at the war for the escapade of the thing, as if courage were just disdain of fear. So they made it look, and some of them kept it up. Aubrey Herbert, receiving notice of his rejection for military service, entered the army by obtaining a uniform of the Irish Guards, and falling in step with that regiment as it passed him in the street. Raymond Asquith was killed at the Somme. The gallantry of his manner of dying – chatting and smoking so his men would not be afraid – gave the final burnish to his reputation and served Churchill with another opportunity for the sort of eulogy he had exercised the year before upon the death of Rupert Brooke.

Unacceptable as a soldier, Farrer went to work for the civil service, at the newly formed Ministry of Information. This was the government's propaganda department, set up in 1917 with John Buchan at its head and, at its extremities, the pantheon of Edwardian writers. Just as the most beautiful gardens were set to cabbages, so were men like Arnold Bennett, Thomas Hardy, H. G. Wells, Arthur Quiller-Couch, Rudyard Kipling, G. K. Chesterton, Robert Bridges, Henry Newbolt, John Galsworthy and Sir Arthur Conan-Doyle now set to propaganda, producing in quantity such pamphlets as 'The Psychology of the Kaiser', 'The Spectre of Navalism', 'Frightfulness in Theory and Practice', 'Slavery in Europe'. Five tons of documents emerged from this ministry, and some of them were written by Reginald Farrer. The war and his work for it, he later wrote to Osbert Sitwell, left him with a nauseated horror of 'lies and humbug, journalism,

Christianity, domesticity, dullness and European civilisation in general'. The only way to negotiate its madness, he said, had been to:

> make oneself drunk with the DAILY MAIL, so as to live through the dreadful drunkenness of everyone else... Let no one say I didn't do my best. But how greatly I loathed myself, and life, and everything all the time.

Farrer had carried out his war work in this condition. John Buchan sent him out to cover the three fronts of the European war, and report back in letters Buchan praised as 'first class'. The book that these became, *The Void of War*, takes a view of German manhood that would have found high favour in the offices of the *Daily Mail*. German prisoners-of-war appear as:

> low, chétif, weaselly types... and the look in their eyes is like a bad smell. It lowers and slinks, it is furtively and coldly malignant. This is not a journalistic flourish of imagination, because they were boches: it is what I met as I passed them.

It is worth mentioning in this context that James Anson Farrer was appalled by the war against Germany from the outset and, by resigning the presidency of the Skipton Liberal Association, had made his objection felt. But there is no evidence from this period to suggest an improvement in relations between father and son. In *The Void of War*, the sight of a black-clad orphan prompts the sole reflection, 'but how much better than to grow up and wish in vain you were one'. Osbert Sitwell tells us that his cousin now referred to his parents at all times as 'The Watsons', for their habit, defined in Sherlock Holmes' assistant, of coming late to the wrong conclusion, from the wrong deductions, 'still sure of the essential rightness of their methods'.

Farrer's world was not wholly greyed over by the war. He could have mornings like the one he spent with Sitwell and a Madame Vandervelde, in March of 1918, drinking peach brandy in the garden of an inn near Bath. When the bottle was nearly done, they 'staged an impromptu bachannale [sic]', prancing around the garden with wreaths of ivy on their heads, Farrer in Sitwell's regimental overcoat which, enormously too long for him, trailed out behind on the grass, 'as if he were a child dressed up in the clothes of his parents. More than ever he resembled an oriental version of Silenus.'

Sitwell believed, as many did, that Farrer's interest in the Far East arose from his 'oriental' appearance: an opinion illustrating the profound ignorance of the Orient that Farrer often deplored in his countrymen. Only an Englishman could think Farrer looked Chinese.

***

How much there was to keep him in England may be gauged by the haste of his departure. The war ended on 11 November 1918; on 31 January he was on a boat out of Liverpool harbour, having made all the arrangements and procured the necessary funds and permissions for a two-year plant collecting expedition to Upper Burma.

It is a miracle that this ill-conceived trip, generated by despair and shaped by compromise, ever managed to take place at all. Farrer had written to Bayley-Balfour back in August, sending him a rare map he had managed to acquire of the Sino-Burmese border, and proposing, in the event of peace, an expedition to the area north of Putao, where a mountainous and forested triangle divides the Mekong and the Salween rivers. Bayley-Balfour wrote back his approval, saying that if he could find a base to the north of this region, where Forrest and Kingdon-Ward had not yet penetrated, it would prove 'the finest unexplored area in the world for plants'. 'Twenty men working for twenty years would never exhaust it,' he claimed. Yet by Christmas Farrer was still unsure if he was going to Burma or to Bhutan; nor had he found a companion. And now he was in hospital, having his appendix out. The proximity of this event to his departure date does not seem to have perturbed him: 'I await to hear from my beloved Purdom that he's willing to go,' he wrote from his hospital bed as though from a hotel.

In the event, Purdom was not willing. The most likely explanation is that the Chinese forestry department wouldn't release him at such short notice. But one cannot dismiss the possibility that this shy and reticent man had read *On the Eaves of the World* and noticed the ripening campness of those parts of it that dealt with himself – the unresisted opportunities to dwell upon his handsome physique, his 'Nordic Beauty', or to describe those occasions when Farrer dressed him up in antique Chinese armour or furs bought from a Russian trader. Whether or not this tone betrayed the truth of their relationship is immaterial: Purdom may not have liked it in either case. At any rate, he stayed in China, and died there in 1921.

After a failed attempt to join up with the professional collector R. F. Cooper, in Bhutan, Farrer was left with the prospect plainly before him of going to Burma on his own. But then he received a visit at his nursing home from a kind young man called Euan Cox. Cox was the son of an industrialist whom Farrer had met while they had both been working at the ministry. He had some leanings towards horticulture and other, more urgent ones, away from the Cox family jute business, where his presence was keenly awaited now that the war was over. Within half an hour, Farrer had persuaded him to defer his fate and to come with him to Burma for the first year.

This first season in Burma with Cox was in every way a different experience from his time in Kansu with Purdom, and chiefly because of the differences between those two men. As we know, Purdom's practical expertise was limitless. Superior in experience to Farrer, he was nevertheless his social inferior, and his character was one in which masterfulness and deference were mixed in the most satisfactory proportions.

With Cox, it was the other way around: he would neither fill his position nor know his place. Moreover, being younger and inexperienced, it was reasonable for him to expect the practised collector to take care of him. For Farrer, this year was a test of character, and he failed it with flying colours. This we know, because one of the many ways Cox differed from Purdom was that Cox kept a diary.

***

There were few triumphs that season. The region of Upper Burma, so accommodating on the map, was infested in reality with unforeseen political and geographical problems: a hot, jungly, leech-filled country without roads, and thick with restrictions of access that prevented them from getting north to Putao and finding the 'centre to work out of' that Bayley-Balfour had established as the *sine qua non* of success. They had to remain to the south, near Hpimaw, in an area that Forrest and Kingdon-Ward had already picked over and where they were both still sitting, unable to go north just as Farrer was. In April, some of Forrest's collectors came over from the neighbouring mountain, provoking such a swarm of furious letters from Farrer that the persecuted Forrest eventually wrote to Bayley-Balfour to explain that there was nothing he could do:

> I have just had another [letter] dated 25/5 in which he bewails the foregathering of the three of us on almost one spot... He, Farrer, is working with only 2 Ghurkha orderlies – given him by the superintendent of Police here – as collectors! How he manages I often wonder, as I find I cannot do much good with less than 15 or 20! Must be a gift! We have come to a temporary agreement that neither of us shall trespass beyond the frontier, but I cannot promise that will hold good.

At the end of May, Farrer and Cox set out to climb up the Hpimaw pass, to get up to higher ground and make an encampment there. It rained all the time, confining them for days to the camp and one another's company, and making the plants they did find – some exceptional rhododendrons and a magnolia as superb, Farrer said, as *M. campbelli* but flowering later in the season, and 'laughing at sleet and rain' – almost impossible to dry. It was Farrer, not Forrest or Kingdon-Ward, who now found *Nomocharis farreri*, (syn. *N. pardanthina var. farreri*) the purple-spattered lily-like bulb, but even this, and the sight of it growing in lake-like profusion in a high alpine meadow, could hardly redeem the failures. Tension built between Cox and Farrer. It is plain from Cox's diary that Farrer expected from him the same standard of service that he was used to getting from Purdom, but didn't get it: Cox was slow and tentative. He spoilt the photographic plates and dug up the wrong things, and failed to brace the striking Burmese bearers. Nor could he calm Farrer down as Purdom had managed to do. After the visit from Forrest's men, Farrer fumed and paced and talked to himself. He began to drink.

To add to Cox's sins of ineptitude, he now revealed a fatal tendency: he was bookish, and nursed writerly longings. To Cox himself, this seemed a great personal strength and a potential agent of cohesion between them. Farrer, he figured – 'the Master' – could help him with his writing. 'I must make the most of the shining hour & take lessons in how to write English from Reginald,' he advised his diary. But, as any reader of that document must notice at once, this development of Cox – from Cox, the presser of plants and packer of trunks, into Cox, the young man of letters, writer of sonnets and critic of novels – affected Farrer's mood directly, tripping it from sullen to poisonous. Almost immediately after this entry, their relationship guttered. As the rain drilled on the canvas of their tent, pinned high on the shoulder of one of a thousand unpeopled dark green mountains that corrugate the earth at the Sino-Burmese frontier, they started to bicker about books. Cox was 'not greatly taken' with *Northanger Abbey*. Only people with true Literary Judgement liked *Northanger Abbey*, Farrer returned, testily. Sensing the implication, Cox retaliated in his diary. 'L.J. is a god with clay feet,' he huffed, 'people who quote and stand by L.J. usually don't think for themselves.' That there might be any connection between Farrer's mood and his own essay into writing seems to have escaped Cox entirely. In September, back at Hpimaw, with cordiality almost worn away between them, he decided to write a novel. In the unravelling of the next days, despite the wild touchiness of Farrer over small misdeeds, and a conspicuous increase in the production of blank verse and articles from Farrer's end of the tent, Cox's account of the situation remains miraculously unpolluted by the least trickle of understanding:

11 September: worked at the Immortal Work and little else. It is certainly beginning to come along now.

12 September: R[eginald]. has been more annoying today than I have ever seen him. Some day soon I will beat him up. He has the superiority in brains but I can at least hurt him bodily & if I begin his face will be a fruity sight.

13 September: …I have been having a rest from the masterpiece. R & I quite good friends again.

They were not. The complaints about Farrer, faint and widely scattered in the first part of Cox's diary, now lie in considerable accumulations. With Cox he is 'querulous and abusive', worryingly egoistic, peevish, petty, 'noisy and absurd', and irretrievably drunk. 'I am afraid he is too old to learn when he has had enough.' In his dealings with the local officials he has got 'an extraordinary bad way with him & frequently ignores the most obvious civilities'... 'Everything is taken for granted & all done for us is his due not act of kindness.'

By October Cox was longing for home. 'I can't say how I am looking forward to being alone again. I don't know what I should say to Ernest about it all... It is odd that a man with so many brains should think himself a combination of God, Demosthenes and George Moore all rolled into one.'

In December, after the seed harvest, Cox and Farrer met up with Frank Kingdon-Ward and travelled back to Rangoon with him. The two collectors discussed the possibility of joint expeditions to Russia, by aeroplane, or to Nepal; then, after a terrible Boxing-Day row between them, of which Cox, observing, wrote 'If I had been K-W I would have hit him,' they all parted. Cox went home to a life free of jute, but so haunted by Farrer that he wrote three reverential books around him*.

---

*Farrer's Last Journey (1926), The Plant Introductions of Reginald Farrer (1930), and Plant-hunting in China (1945)

Farrer went up to Maymo, outside Mandalay, to pass the winter in 'a charming little house' there, waiting for the next season.

That winter brought only dispiriting news. The rupee rose against the pound, doubling his expenses for the year in view. Bayley-Balfour wrote to say that many of the Hpimaw plants had been either dead on arrival, or discovered already, like the magnolia (*M. rostrata*), found the year before by Forrest. He also learned that he had had better reason than he could have imagined to deplore Forrest's presence on 'his' patch earlier that year. Forrest's employer was the seed-seller A.K. Bulley, also one of Farrer's main sponsors in Burma. For Bulley, labour costs and income tax were rising, cinema had killed the flower show, and the anticipated post-war market for hardy plants was failing to revive. Forrest's seeds arrived first, providing Bulley with more potential plants than he could ever sell, and so, being a man of more prudence than imagination, he pulled his money out from Farrer.

The last piece of bad news was from Derrick Milner, a young man known to Farrer and Cox by his nickname, the 'Beautiful Boy'. He had engaged to be Farrer's companion for the next season. Now, suddenly, he was backing out and taking with him his contribution to the season's expenses. Why? There is nothing to prove that a word with Cox put him off, but, in view of all that followed, it is hard to avoid the surmise.

In shock and fear, Farrer wrote to Bayley-Balfour. Would he desist from behaving 'as if it were only original sin on my part that debars me from going North. In fact I am doing so, as far as I can get. Only not even a Botanical explorer... is exempt from the human frailty of requiring food.' He implored Bayley-Balfour, and his deputy, Smith, to scratch him up some more financial support. He anticipated considerable expense over the next year: the range of mountains he had in mind, about 120 miles north of Hpimaw, was a twelve-week journey, there and back, away from any possible base. He would need forty mules to carry 'every *atom* of food, for me and all the staff, for the whole season'. Unless more money came, he warned them, his position threatened to become quite unpleasant.

***

Why didn't he go home? Every fresh development urged it, and he must have known from the last season that most of the plants in the area would be unsuitable for cultivation in England. He could have counted Milner's defection the final straw and returned without dishonour, as some of his friends advised. In a letter to Aubrey Herbert, he answers the question:

> What else would there be for me better to do if I did follow dear Beb's* advice, and come home? In plain fact, I can't very well go on living at Ingleborough while the Family rule and I have no means or wish to live anywhere else in England. Unless you want a lodgekeeper... considering prospects, I do not see that I can do better than make plant-collecting my business in life, and be only thankful for the miraculous mercy that turns one's greatest pleasure into a possible livelihood.

It was a way of saying he had nowhere else to go.

In the spring of 1920, the descriptive term for an Englishman travelling in Burma with a dozen muleteers, a groom, an interpreter, three domestic staff

*Herbert Asquith, brother of Raymond

and two Ghurkha orderlies was still 'alone'. It was the right word for Farrer, who loved company and, in the days of his European travels, would beguile the tedium of a long journey by making everyone talk in rhyming couplets. He had never made any of the travel arrangements himself, and had to now; nor was he a man with a talent for personnel management: it was he who, in China, had sent his Ma-fu thousands of feet down the Himalayan pass to fetch *Northanger Abbey,* and when this man, who couldn't read in any language, struggled back with *Emma*, showed little clemency.

He headed north for the tiny hill station of Fort Hertz, then east, over the Irrawaddy river, to another tiny station called Nyitadi. The journey was troublesome and slow. His muleteers struck at the Irrawaddy and he had to re-supply himself with mules. When he set up camp above Nyitadi, he found the hills, sold to him as limestone and free of bamboo scrub, full of bamboo and granitic. Of the three passes he explored, only one had good plants on it, few of them new. It rained exceptionally that year, rain upon rain, week upon week. Farrer must have realised that this was hardly a propitious climate for plants that would thrive in England.

Work did for company in his porous shack. He painted the flowers he had collected and worked on two books, one a novel, optimistically entitled *The Empty House*. His correspondence suggests that something happened to him up there, a kind of lightening and freshening of the spirits. It may have been the discovery that he could cope alone, as he feared he might not; or just the effect of whisky – which was sent out to him by the caseful – upon despair, but his letters show a new lightheadedness and looseness. He wrote generally of his enjoyment of the season, and how much he pre-ferred it to the previous one with Cox; sending these tidings also to Cox, in one of many bullying, apolo-getic, effeminate and notably unstable letters which Cox now received, and would show to no one.

What a comfort it was, wrote Farrer,

> *not* to have my dear nephew grizzling on my heels... How I do look forward to our motor-trip next year on the Continong [sic]: I feel you will be absolutely *ideal* where comfort is prevalent.

During the seed harvest he got a letter from Herbert, and he wrote back, nosing him, like a dog with a stick, with his future plans. He had two things to offer: a meeting-up in Peking and the free disposal of his heart. Would Aubrey and Mary please find him a wife, one that they would find acceptable?

> Find me a fair one, please, not particular about looks; and assist my diffidence in the matter… as you know, such hotness as I can muster is always rather in such heart as I've got rather than in my blood (but)… I have now got quite a lot to give, in the way of happiness, if both parties play the game.

He added that he particularly hungered for children, though not especially for the 'methods of procuring them'. To the observer, this proposal lacks the look of a thing that has been examined from all sides, but it makes an eloquent declaration of love. A wife of Herbert's choice would have, in Farrer's mind, the inestimable virtue of conducting affection back to the sole source; to surrender this task to Aubrey was, in effect, to humbly ask him for a proxy.

As it turned out, there was nothing long-term about Farrer's prospects. He fell ill in October, with a cough and chest pains. When ill, it was his habit to dose himself with the entire contents of his medicine box, taken indiscriminately with whisky; but this time he worsened, got more breathless, fainted more often. His servant, Bhanje Bhanju, who had been with him all the time in Burma, now ran to Konglu for help. He made a week's journey in three days, not resting on the way or upon arrival in Konglu, but Farrer died anyway.

Writing through the offices of an interpreter, Bhanju explained how, from the 14 October, his 'breafvery and honesty officer... discontinued to take his food except soda water, wiskly and medicines for his benefit but it has been unsuccessful at least and without giving any pain and trouble to us he breathe his last on the morning of 17th October 1920.' Farrer's last conscious act was to write a commendation of his staff.

Six coolies carried him down to Nyitadi and buried him there. They left his seeds and his novels in the tent, but they sent his diaries, once described by him as 'the best English biography', back to his mother, who cut them up with scissors. His family put up a little memorial, like a birdbath in one of his gardens, and wrote upon it, with sublime consistency, that he had died for 'Plants and Duty'.

Aubrey Herbert died in 1922, of an infection. There is no reference in his diaries to Reginald Farrer, or to the event of his death.

SELECT BIBLIOGRAPHY

Works by Reginald Farrer:

On the Eaves of the World 2 Vols. (Edward Arnold, 1917)
The Rainbow Bridge (Edward Arnold, 1921)
The English Rock Garden (T.C. and E.C. Jack, 2 vols, 1919)
In a Yorkshire Garden (Edward Arnold, 1909)
My Rock Garden (4th impression, Edward Arnold, 1907)

Reginald Farrer: Dalesman, Planthunter, Gardener, Edited by John Illingworth and Jane Routh (Centre for North-West Regional Studies, University of Lancaster, 1991)
Victorian Gardens, Brent Elliott (B.T. Batsford, 1986)
The Man who was Greenmantle, Margaret FitzHerbert (John Murray, 1983)
Raymond Asquith: Life and Letters, Edited by John Jolliffe (Michael Russell Publishing, 1998)
Plant Hunting in China, E.H. Cox (1945)
The Anthology of Garden Writing, Ursula Buchan (Croom Helm, 1986)

E.A. Bowles: My Garden in Spring (1914)

On crocuses:

'The older form of *C. korolkowii* from further East is a washy little imitation of these better forms, greenish on the back, rather the colour you sometimes find on the outside of the yolk of a hard-boiled egg, and suggestive of dirty metal – German Silver, or Brittania metal, "which goes green and smells nasty", as Mrs. Brown knew by experience...'

'...*C. lacteus* is an ivory white in colour, distinct from any other, and you can see it is a yellow turned white, reminding one of that beautiful softened shade of white that in old age replaces red hair of the shade euphemistically called auburn, but colloquially carrots or ginger.'

Marion Cran: The Garden Beyond (1937)

'Yellow then he brought in sheaves from our garden to hold among the blue beds that we might see the effect; soft primrose and lemon yellow – nothing harsh or glaring, not marigolds, montbretias, or any such hot flowers. Just as the touch of a clapper upon the sullen metal of a voiceless bell wakes it into thrilling sound, her blue was struck by the yellow into vibrant tone. Madonna lilies had been ice-cold; primrose and citron were gentle and yet valiant.'

and **Wind Harps (1929)**
'...through May and June opens the peony harvest; there are single and double forms in every shade and shape, cups of shell-pink filled with a creamy tangle, huge perfumed balls of satin petals incurved like great chrysanthemums; flat water-lily saucers of waxen white crowded with gold; bundles of cream and rose baby-ribbon petals, as dainty as a sea-anemone, sumptuous chalices of lacquered red, and big red mops coarse and good-hearted, the hoydens of the genus.'

Vita Sackville-West: Some Flowers (1927).
'I suppose her (*Tulipa clusiana*, called the lady tulip) alleged femineity is due to her elegance and neatness, with her little white shirt so simply tucked inside her striped jacket, but she is really more like a slender boy, a slim little officer dressed in a parti-coloured uniform of the Renaissance.'

'(*Rosa moyesii*) is a Chinese rose, and looks it. If ever a plant reflected all that we had ever felt about the delicacy, lyricism, and design of a Chinese drawing, *Rosa moyesii* is that plant. We might well expect to meet her on a Chinese printed paper-lining to a tea-chest of the time of Charles II, when wall-papers first came to England, with a green parrot quite out of all proportions, perching on her slender branches.'

'For when it (*Fritillaria meleagris*) grows at all, it can grow as thick as a blue-bell, sombre and fuscous, singularly unsuitable to the water-meadows and the willows of an Oxfordshire or a Hampshire stream. In wine-making countries one has seen the musty heaps of crushed discarded grape-skins after the juice has been pressed from them. Their colour is then almost exactly that of the meadow fritillary.'

Andrew Young: A Retrospect of Flowers (1950)
'Moschatel is seldom noticed, being a small delicate plant that often shelters under Dog Mercury leaves... Its square flower-head has four faces like a clock-tower, but also overlying them is a fifth face like a sun-dial, so that it goes one better than the cherubim described by Milton, "Four faces each had, like a double Janus." '

Edward A. Bunyard: The Anatomy of Dessert (1933).
'There is but little doubt that a dark chapter in melonic history lies concealed in the mists of antiquity. I suspect a family scandal, a *tertium quid*, and, if I may so far offend the delicacy of my readers, I would hint that a vegetable marrow played the dastard part...'

'...I have a preference for the green-fleshed varieties such as

Emerald gem; their cool transparent jade interiors are attractive to the eye, whereas the salmon yellow of the ordinary melon is a rather meretricious colour.'

'At the same season Buerré Giffard (pear) ripens, but any trained eye can see that this is all wrong: the red cheek is not the healthy flush of nature nor the yellow ground without artifice – it is too obviously copied from those marble fruits which decorate alabaster bowls in Florentine shops.'

'Of the gathering of peaches much might be said; let it suffice that they are neither pinched nor pulled off, but rather stroked off. A fond and delicate hand is applied, and a gentle rotatory movement should suffice if they are ripe. As the shoot on which they grow usually requires to be pruned off later on, I would rather take away a small piece, in the manner that grapes are cut, than suffer those tell-tale patches of brown under the skin which indicate that lust – rather than love – has directed their gathering.

'Nor should the butler's fingers intervene.'

Author's note: All the writers quoted here refer to Farrer in their works.

ACKNOWLEDGEMENTS

Many thanks to Mr Rupert Christiansen and to the many other people who have offered assistance and advice, especially Mr Trevor Wilshire, Mr John Mitchell, Sir Peter Smithers, Miss Claudia FitzHerbert, Professor Luciano Petech, Sir Matthew Farrer, Dr and Mrs John Farrer, Dr John Page and Professor Gren Lucas. I am most grateful to the staff of the Lindley Library, the Library of the Royal Botanic Gardens, Edinburgh, the Balliol College Library, and to Mrs Elizabeth Turner at the department of Western Manuscripts in the Bodleian Library. I would particularly like to thank Mrs Bridget Grant, Mr and Mrs Gwilym Slimm and Mr Michael Upward for their immense generosity and hospitality.

Grateful acknowledgement is made to Mrs Bridget Grant, Mrs Charles Brand, and the Earl of Oxford and Asquith for permission to quote from family documents, and to the Library of the Royal Botanic Gardens, Edinburgh, for permission to quote from documents held in its collection.